PHILOSOPHY
Rocks!

PHILOSOPHY Rocks!

By Stephen Law

Illustrated by Daniel Postgate

HYPERION
NEW YORK

First published under the title *The Philosophy Files*
in Great Britain by Orion Children's Books,
a division of the Orion Publishing Group Ltd.

Text copyright © 2000 by Stephen Law
Illustrations copyright © 2000 by Daniel Postgate

Printed in the United States of America
First American Edition, 2002
1 3 5 7 9 10 8 6 4 2
This book is set in 11.5-point Joanna.

ISBN 0-7868-1699-6
Visit www.volobooks.com

For Taryn

Lots of people helped me with this book. Sophie Walker (age 13) gave me some very valuable comments. I would also like to thank these adults: Taryn Storey, Justine Burley, Mick O'Neill, Miranda Fricker, Geoff Mees, and Janice Thomas. Special thanks are due to my mum, Maureen.

Contents

Big Questions

Here I am, climbing a mountain.

One reason I like to climb is that,
while I sit taking in or letting out the rope and my partner is climbing, I can look at the scenery and think.

What do I think about? Well, being so far up above everything can give you a quite different view of the world. Rather than being caught up in my day-to-day life, I usually end up thinking about questions like these: Where did the universe come from? Is there life after death? Does God exist? What makes things right or wrong? and Could my whole life have been a dream?

These are *philosophical* questions. They are some of the biggest and most exciting questions that have ever been asked. Humankind has been grappling with them for thousands of years.

I'm sure you've asked such questions yourself. If you have, then this book is for you.

Of course, some religious books claim to have the answers to these and other philosophical questions. But it's important to realize that this is *not* a religious book. It is a philosophy book. It's a book that encourages you to question and figure things out for yourself.

The book is made up of eight chapters. Each chapter looks at a different philosophical question. You don't have to start at the beginning of the book. You can jump in wherever you like, depending on which question first grabs your attention.

And remember, the important thing in philosophy is to think for yourself. You certainly don't have to agree with me about everything. In fact, you may find that I have made mistakes and taken a wrong turn here and there.

Many philosophical questions can be a bit frightening to think about. That's one reason why some people don't like to think about them—they like to stay where they feel safe. But if you are anything like me, you will enjoy the challenge, excitement, and sense of vertigo that thinking philosophically can bring. So get ready for a journey to the outer limits of thought.

For we are about to open . . .

PHILOSOPHY ROCKS!

Question 1

What is real?

The world around me
Here's my study.

As you can see, I'm working on a computer. On my desk is a bowl full of apples. There are also some Tibetan singing bowls that I bought when I visited India. Beside the desk is a bookcase full of books. There's a fireplace with some rather dusty dried flowers in it. On the other side of the room is a window. You can see some trees and clouds and the sun shining outside. Beyond them are the spires of Oxford.

Now, most people, if you were to ask them, *what is reality?* would probably say that reality is what I'm experiencing all around me right now. The world of desks and chairs, trees and clouds: that's reality; that's the real world.

But not everyone would agree with this. In particular, Plato wouldn't agree. According to Plato, what I see around me is actually just shadows. The real world is hidden from our five senses. It cannot be tasted, seen, smelled, heard, or touched.

So what is this hidden world like? According to Plato, it is quite wonderful.

It contains everything that is essential and perfect. It has always been there and will always be there. It is the place from which we came. And it is the place to which we go when we die.

Plato also says that if we want knowledge, it is to this world beyond the shadows that we must look. Our five senses cannot give us knowledge of how things *really* are. So how do we find out how things are beyond the shadows? As we will see, Plato argues that the only way to genuine knowledge is through the use of reason.

This chapter is about Plato's world beyond the shadows. Does it really exist?

Plato

Who was Plato?

Plato was born nearly two and a half thousand years ago, in ancient Greece. He is perhaps the most famous of all philosophers. In fact, Plato is considered by many to be the father of philosophy.

A good place to start with Plato is with a story—a story first told by Plato all those

years ago (I've changed the story a bit, but it's essentially the same).

Plato's story of the cave

There is a cave. And at the very bottom of this cave are kept some prisoners. The prisoners are kept chained up, facing a wall. They are never allowed to turn and see what is behind them. So the prisoners spend their entire lives looking only at the wall.

Then, one day, one of the prisoners—let's call him "Alf"—is released. He is made to turn around and look up.

At first, Alf is blinded by a brilliant light. It hurts his eyes. But after a while Alf's eyes start to adjust.

As his eyes become accustomed to the light, Alf begins to see that up above the prisoners and behind them is a fire. It was this fire that first blinded him. And between the fire and the prisoners is a path.

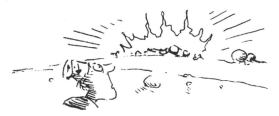

The path is used by the jailers. Alf can see that, as the jailers walk along the path carrying objects, the objects they carry cast shadows down onto the wall in front of the prisoners.

Now, Alf has never seen a real object before. When he was a prisoner, he could see only the shadows that were cast on the wall. So, like all the other prisoners, he ended up supposing that these shadows were the real objects. He mistook what he saw on the wall for reality.

But now Alf can see how he and the other prisoners had been fooled. He now understands that what he had earlier taken to be the real world was merely a parade of shadows. He realizes that the *real* world had been hidden from him.

A little later, some of the jailers lead Alf from the cave into the sunlight outside. The brightness of the light again blinds him at first. But gradually Alf's eyes adjust. Finally, he recognizes the sun.

Now, Alf is a kind man. Not surprisingly, he feels very sorry for the other prisoners he has left behind in the cave. So he decides to return down into the depths to tell them what he has seen, to explain to them how things *really* are. He feels sure they will want to know all about his journey into the real world.

But when Alf reaches the bottom of the cave, his eyes are no longer accustomed to the dark. He stumbles. He bumps into things. So the other prisoners think that Alf's journey has made him blind.

Then things get worse. When Alf starts to explain to them how things *really* are, they don't want to listen. They are happily engrossed watching the shadows in front of them. They tell him to shut up. They act just like grumpy people act when their favorite TV program has been interrupted.

But Alf won't give up. He wants to help them. So he keeps on trying to tell them all about the hidden world up above them. Then the prisoners get really angry. They start shouting at him. "Just *go away!*" they yell. "Stop pestering us with your stupid talk! *We* can see perfectly well how things are—it's *you* who's blind!"

And when Alf still won't give up, the prisoners throw rocks at him. They drive him away. And so the prisoners waste away their lives watching shadows. They never do find out the truth.

The world beyond the shadows

You've probably guessed that Plato's story about the prisoners in the cave is not just a story. Plato is trying to tell us something. But what is he trying to tell us?

Well, *we* are the prisoners in the cave. And the things we see around us are those shadows on the cave wall. Just like the prisoners in the cave, we are taken in by the shadows. We mistake the shadows for reality. We suppose that what we can see is the real world. But the real world cannot be seen.

Souls

Plato also argued that each of us has a soul. He argued that it is to this real world that the soul goes when we die. So death is really nothing to be afraid of. When you die, your soul doesn't stop existing. It carries on. It goes to a much better place.

Heaven

A number of religions talk about Heaven. Heaven is where we are supposed to go when we die (at least if we have been good).

Now, Plato's idea of a perfect world—the real world that lies beyond the shadows—certainly does sound a bit like this modern idea of Heaven, doesn't it? And that's not entirely a coincidence. Over the centuries, religious thinkers have read Plato and borrowed from his ideas. The modern idea of Heaven—in particular, the modern Christian idea of Heaven—has been shaped in part by Plato's ideas.

C. S. Lewis and the Shadowlands

Plato's thinking has influenced our thinking about the world right up to the present day. In particular, Plato's philosophy has had an important part to play in shaping Western philosophy, religion, art, and literature.

Let me give you one example. You may have heard of C. S. Lewis. C. S. Lewis was a Christian. He wrote children's books about a land called Narnia. The best-known book about Narnia is called *The Lion, the Witch and the Wardrobe*.

The final book about Narnia is called *The Last Battle*. In its closing pages, Narnia comes to an end. The land is covered by sea, and the sun is put out. All the good creatures from Narnia pass through a door into an extraordinary new land.

Finding themselves in this new land, the children whom the Narnia stories are about wonder where they can be. Parts of the new land seem like the Narnia they remember, only far more wonderful. And parts of it seem like the England they remember, only, again, far more wonderful.

Then one of the characters in the story explains to the children that the Narnia and England that they remember were not the *real* Narnia or the *real* England. They were just *shadows* of the real world in which they now find themselves. This real world has always existed and will always exist, and is as different from the old Narnia and the old England as a real object is different from its shadow.

Finally, on the very last page of *The Last Battle*, the children wonder how they could have ended up in this wonderful place. They are afraid they might be made to leave. But then it is explained to them that they are actually all dead—they were killed in a railway accident. They have now passed over from what C. S. Lewis calls the *Shadowlands* into the real world where they will live happily ever after. Their old lives were but a dream: this is the morning.

As you have probably guessed, C. S. Lewis borrowed this idea of the real world beyond the shadows—the real world to which we go when we die—from Plato. In fact, if you read *The Last Battle* carefully, you will discover that near the end of the story one of the characters actually tells the children that it's all in Plato.

An invisible world

So Plato believes that this world—the world that you and I are experiencing right now—isn't the real world. We live merely in the Shadowlands, as Lewis calls them.

The world we see around us might seem like the real world, but it's not.

The real world is invisible. It lies beyond what we can taste, see, smell, hear, and touch.

But why did Plato suppose that these are merely the Shadowlands, and that the real world lies beyond? What's the philosophy, the argument behind these extraordinary views? That's what we will now explore.

The form of beauty

Here are five beautiful things:

They are a beautiful flower, a beautiful person, a beautiful mountain, a beautiful sunset, and a beautiful garden. Of course, these five beautiful things are different in many ways (for example, the person has hair, and the mountain doesn't). Still, each is beautiful.

But what is *beauty* itself? While each of these things may be a beautiful thing, it seems that none is beauty itself. Beauty itself seems to be something else—a further thing that exists in addition to all the particular things that there are.

Plato calls this further thing—beauty itself—the *Form* of beauty. He says that what makes particular beautiful things beautiful is the fact that they share this Form.

Other Forms

According to Plato, it's not just beautiful things that share a common Form. Beautiful things are just one type of thing. There are many other types of thing. Take chairs, for example.

Chairs are a type of thing. Despite their many differences, there is something that all chairs have in common—the something that *makes* them chairs. According to Plato, this "something" is another Form: *the Form of the chair.*

This Form of the chair exists in addition to all the particular chairs that there are.

There are many other kinds of Forms, according to Plato. For example, large things (such as elephants, mountains, and giant redwood trees) are a type of thing. To them corresponds the Form of largeness. Actions that are just (an example of a just action would be when a judge and jury fairly punish someone for a terrible crime) are yet another type of thing. To them corresponds the Form of justice. And so on.

In fact, if we follow Plato's reasoning here, it seems there must be a Form for *every* type of thing there is. There must be a Form of the flower, a Form of red things, a Form of the rabbit, a Form of the house, a Form of the cheeseburger, even.

So what are Plato's Forms like?

The Forms are perfect

First of all, *the Forms are perfect.* Take beauty, for example. Any beautiful thing that you might experience will not be *perfectly* beautiful. It could always be more beautiful than it is. But the Form of beauty— beauty itself—is quite perfect. There can't be anything more beautiful than beauty itself, can there?

All the things we see around us are imperfect. All are flawed. All will break or wear out or get moldy. Take beds, for example. Any particular bed that you might happen to see will not be perfect. It could always be more comfortable. It will eventually wear out or break. But, again, the Form of the bed is quite perfect. Each Form is the one and only perfect example of things of that type.

The Forms are invisible

Second, *the Forms are not the sort of thing that one can taste, see, smell, hear, or touch.* Nothing that we can experience is ever perfect. So the Form of the chair, being perfect, is not something that we can experience. We can see particular, imperfect chairs, of course, but the Form of the chair is invisible.

The Forms are more real

Third, the Forms are *more real* than are the particular things that we experience around us. For those particular things depend for their existence on the Forms.

Take a look at the tree in my backyard. Throughout the day this tree casts many shadows. It is also reflected in puddles and windowpanes.

These fleeting images of the tree are distorted and imperfect copies of the tree. They depend on the tree being there for their existence. Without the tree, there can be no shadows or reflections of it.

Similarly, without the Form of the tree there can be no particular trees. Those trees we see around us—including that tree in my yard—depend on the Form of the tree for their existence: they are imperfect shadows or reflections of this Form.

And the same goes for all the other objects we see around us. They are not the *real* objects. The real objects are the Forms, of which the objects we see are but fleeting shadows or reflections.

The Forms are eternal and changeless

According to Plato, the Forms are eternal. They have always been there and always will be there. While particular beautiful things may come and go, beauty itself remains.

The Forms are also *changeless*. Of course, the world around us is changing all the time. Chairs and tables warp, bend, and break. Plants and animals grow, wither, and die. The weather varies from day to day. The seasons come and go. Mountains eventually tumble into the sea. Everything is shifting. But according to Plato, the Forms never change.

You might wonder about this. Take beauty, for example. Don't we consider different things beautiful at different times? For example, our current ideal of a beautiful person is someone who is thin, but not so long ago, heavier people were considered more beautiful.

Fashions change. What at one time might be considered beautiful later generations may find vulgar or even downright ugly. So if there is a Form of beauty, doesn't it change over time?

Not according to Plato. He thought that while fashion may change, beauty itself does not. Real beauty is always the same. It's only our ability to recognize it that varies.

The supreme Form

So there you have it: the world we see around us is not the real world. The real world is a hidden world of perfect, changeless, and eternal Forms.

But there is one last Form that we still need to put into place. There are many Forms. So the Forms themselves are a type of thing. So there must also be a Form of the Forms.

What is the Form of the Forms like? Well, what do all the Forms have in common? They all exist and they are all perfect. So the Form of the Forms is the Form of *existence and perfection*.

Plato called this supreme Form the *Form of the Good*.

The arrangement of the Forms

According to Plato, then, the Forms are arranged like this:

At the very top of the pyramid is the Form of the Good. Below the Form of the Good are all the other Forms: the Form of beauty, the Form of the chair, the Form of the table, and so on. And below these Forms are the particular objects that we see around us: particular beds, for example.

Just as the particular chairs, tables, beautiful things, and so on gain what existence and perfection they have from their corresponding Forms, so these forms in turn get what existence and perfection they have from the Form of the Good. So ultimately all existence and

perfection flows down from the Form
of the Good.

In Plato's story about the cave, the Form of
the Good is represented by the sun
shining outside the cave. Just as we sometimes
think of the sun as being that from which
everything ultimately comes (because it makes
night and day, controls the seasons and the weather,
makes the plants grow from which animals in turn feed, and so
on), so the Form of the Good is that from which everything ultimately owes its existence.

God
Plato's idea of the Form of the Good—the Form from which all
existence and perfection flow—sounds much like the modern
idea of God, doesn't it? Many modern religions—in particular,
Christianity, Islam, and Judaism—suppose that God has precisely
this role. God is that to which everything owes its existence and
from which all perfection comes.

Again, this similarity is not completely accidental. This is
another example of how Plato's ideas have helped to shape religious
thinking right up to the present day.

Where does knowledge come from?
We experience the world around us by using our five senses—
taste, sight, smell, hearing, and touch.

But, as we have seen, Plato argues that the world we experience in this way is not the real world. The world that we experience is merely a shadow world.

This is one reason why Plato says that our senses cannot provide us with genuine knowledge. According to Plato, our senses can only deceive us. *Genuine* knowledge is knowledge of the true reality, the world that lies beyond what our five senses reveal. Genuine knowledge is knowledge of the Forms.

So how do we come by knowledge of the Forms, if not by our senses? According to Plato, real knowledge is understood through practicing *philosophy*. Real knowledge comes through the use of *reason*, through *thinking and reflecting*. Those who want real knowledge must ignore the senses. They must close their eyes, put cotton wool in their ears, sit in their favorite armchair, and *think*.

Of course, Plato admits that it is very difficult for philosophers to turn people away from the world of the senses, to convince them that the world we see around us is a mere shadow world, because it does *seem* so real.

The world of the senses can also seem so enticing. We learn to love our senses and the pleasures they bring us: the taste of ice cream, the sound of music, the sight of a beautiful tree. But, according to Plato, there are rarer, higher pleasures—the pleasures that only philosophy can bring. Compared to these higher pleasures, the pleasures of the senses seem very crude and inadequate.

Still, most of us are captivated by our senses. We reject the philosopher who tries to turn us away from the world of the senses and toward the unseen Forms. That's what Plato was trying to warn us about at the end of his story about the cave. We are like the grumpy prisoners who threw rocks at Alf when he tried to turn them away from the shadows and toward the real world.

Science

You might find Plato's views about knowledge rather surprising. Nowadays we think of *science*—physics, chemistry, astronomy, and the rest—as being one of the best routes to knowledge. Science depends ultimately on our five senses: taste, sight, smell, hearing, and touch. Scientists make *observations*. They watch, listen, prod, sniff. Sometimes they even lick. They perform experiments and carefully examine the results. It is upon all these different observations that they base their scientific theories.

Now, you may think, Isn't this sort of *scientific* method one of the best methods of finding out what the world is really like? So isn't Plato wrong to say that our senses cannot give us true knowledge?

Perhaps you are also thinking to yourself: how could people discover anything of any importance by sitting in their favorite armchairs with their eyes shut? Isn't this the *last* way in which we could find out anything about reality? So, again, isn't Plato wrong to say that quiet reflection is the only way to true knowledge? Isn't it quite obvious that no genuine knowledge can be had without the use of the five senses? Surely reason alone is blind. Aren't our senses our only real windows on reality?

It may be that Plato is wrong about the senses not being able to give us knowledge. But perhaps there is *something* to what he says. Maybe it's at least true that some of the most important questions are questions our senses cannot help us answer. Take a look at the following argument.

An argument

Some of the questions that are most important to us are questions that ask, "*What is X?*" For example, we want to know: "What is *justice?*" The question, "What is justice?" is obviously a very important question. We want our society to be just. For example, we want it to have just laws. We want courts to hand out just punishments: punishments that are deserved and that fit the crime (for example, it would hardly be just to execute someone for stealing an apple from a neighbor's tree, right?). So it is very important that we know what justice is. If we don't know what justice is, we won't know how to build a fair and just society.

Other important "*What is X?*" questions are "What is *good?*" "What is *courage?*" "What is *beauty?*" and so on.

Now Plato argued that if you don't yet know what good is, or what courage is, or what beauty is, and you want to find out, it is impossible to find out by observing the world around you.

Take beauty, for example. There may be many beautiful things around you. So why can't you find out what beauty is by observing those things? The problem is this: if you don't *already* know what beauty is, *you won't be able to tell which of the things around you are beautiful.* You won't be able to recognize beauty.

Here's another example (which I just made up—it's not from Plato). Take a look at these different objects:

Suppose I tell you that some of these objects are blibblies and some of them are not. Now, you don't yet know what a blibbly is, do you? You have no idea what it is to be a blibbly. Could you find out what it is to be a blibbly by observing these different objects? No. Obviously not. For you don't yet know which of them are blibblies.

Of course, if I now tell you that something is a blibbly if and only if it is a cube, then you will know which of these objects are blibblies. Now you can tell that just the middle two objects are blibblies. But of course, observing the blibblies won't be of any help *now* because you *already* know what a blibbly is.

It seems, then, that when it comes to answering the question "What is a blibbly?" observing the world around us can't help. Neither, it seems, can it help us answer the questions "What is justice?" "What is beauty?" and so on.

Does this argument convince you? Is Plato right to say that the senses can't help when it comes to answering such questions as "What is justice?" and "What is beauty?" What do you think?

The soul and knowledge of the Forms

As I have already mentioned, Plato believes that each of us has an immortal soul. One reason why the soul is important in Plato's philosophy is that he uses it to explain how we come to have knowledge. As we have just seen, according to Plato, true knowledge comes not from the senses but through the use of reason. But that raises the question: how can reason give us knowledge of the Forms?

Plato's answer to this question seems to be: by somehow reminding us of the Forms. Through reasoning we recollect what we have somehow always known. Our souls existed before our physical bodies were born. Our souls were at that time presented with the Forms. And what knowledge we have of the Forms is actually remembered from back then.

That means, for example, that you are able to recognize beauty now only because you experienced the Form of beauty before you were born. That's also how you are able to recognize a tree. Before you were born, your soul experienced the Form of the tree.

So, when you see a tree now . . .

. . . it reminds you of the Form.

That's how you recognize it's a tree.

Now that I have explained Plato's theory of Forms to you, let's look at two of the best-known criticisms of it.

Criticism 1: The Form of the booger

Plato paints a glorious picture. His perfect, eternal world beyond the shadows certainly sounds wonderful. In fact, it sounds like heaven. Plato certainly seems to think of it as being very heavenly.

Now, one of Plato's arguments for the Forms seems to be this. Whenever there are things that form a *type* of thing (such as beautiful things or chairs or whatever) there is always a *further* thing —a Form—that exists in addition to them. Let's call this argument the *Extra Thing Argument*.

However, there is a problem. Some types of thing are pretty revolting. Take boogers, for example—they are a type of thing.

So by the Extra Thing Argument there must also be a Form of the booger. There must be a *perfect, eternal, and changeless booger*.

But that can't be right, surely? The perfect booger doesn't sound very heavenly, does it? Do we really suppose that the real, heavenly world beyond the shadows contains such disgusting things? I guess not. Certainly, Plato himself didn't seem very keen on the idea.

So the problem is this. Either Plato has to accept that there is a Form of booger (which it seems he wouldn't accept), or else he must admit that the Extra Thing Argument is no good. He can't have it both ways. And if the Extra Thing Argument is no good, then it can't be used to show that *any* Forms exist.

Criticism 2: Too many Forms

One of the most famous criticisms of Plato's theory goes like this.

As I say, Plato seems to use the Extra Thing Argument. Take these beds, for example:

Beds form a type of thing. So, by the Extra Thing Argument, there must be an extra thing—the perfect bed—that exists in addition to all the others, like this:

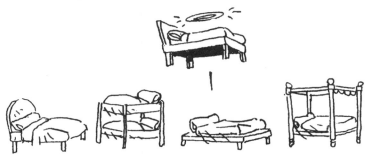

This form is the thing that all particular beds have in common. But now the original beds plus the Form also form a type. They, too, are all beds, so they all have something in common. So by the Extra Thing Argument, we must now add a second Form of the bed:

But of course, the original beds plus the two Forms now also form a type. They too are all beds. So by the Extra Thing Argument there must be a *third* Form of the bed:

There must also be a fourth Form of the bed, and a fifth, and a sixth, and a seventh. The Extra Thing Argument applies again and again without end. So if the Extra Thing Argument is any good, there must actually be an infinite number of Forms of the bed. But that is ridiculous.

Of course, the same problem arises for all the other Forms too. The problem is that Plato can't stop at just one Form for each type of thing. In each case, the Extra Thing Argument seems to require that there be an infinite number of Forms for each type of thing.

If, on the other hand, we deny that there is an infinite number of Forms for each type of thing, as Plato surely would, then we must accept that the Extra Thing Argument is no good. In which case it can't be used to show that there is even one Form for each type of thing.

Do we live in the Shadowlands?
We have now looked at two criticisms of Plato's theory of Forms, both of which seem to be quite good criticisms. But some philosophers argue that these criticisms don't really work. It is also worth remembering that Plato himself knew about these criticisms and wasn't convinced by them. Plato stuck with his theory (as, of course, have many other philosophers, religious thinkers,

writers, artists, and others down through the centuries).

Has Plato convinced you? Is what we see around us the real world? Or are these merely the Shadowlands? What do you think?

I must admit that I am not convinced by Plato's arguments. Still, I have to admit that Plato touches on a feeling that I and many other people seem to have, a feeling that there is more to life, more to reality, than just this. We feel that the *essential* thing—the *important* thing—is hidden.

We feel that if only the curtain could be pulled back, we would see something wonderful. We cannot taste, see, smell, hear, or touch. this "something," but still we feel it is there.

Question 2

Who am I?

Matilda

Meet my Aunt Matilda.

As you can see, Matilda is now quite old: seventy-five years old, in fact. Over the years she has changed a great deal. She has changed physically, of course. She now has white hair whereas once her hair was brown. She now needs a cane and glasses. A very long time ago, when Matilda was a baby, she weighed just a few pounds. Now she weighs over 150 pounds.

Take a look at Matilda's photo album.

When you look through this album, you can see many of these physical changes taking place.

Of course, Matilda has changed mentally, too. Her store of memories has increased over the years. She has also forgotten many things. During her childhood, her intelligence and personality developed very quickly. And even over the past few years, her personality has continued to change a little. For example, she no longer loses her temper when she can't finish a crossword puzzle.

But despite all these physical and psychological changes that Matilda has undergone over the years, it is still the same person who we are presented with in each photograph. It is still Matilda.

Personal identity

Let's now look at the question: what links together that two-year-old, that five-year-old, that ten-year-old, that twenty-five-year-old, that fifty-year-old, that seventy-five-year-old, and, of course, Matilda as she is today as a single person? What *makes* them one and the same person?

This is a question about *personal identity*. More generally, what we want to know is: what does the identity of any given person essentially consist of? This is a question that philosophers have been asking themselves for more than two thousand years. And as we shall see, it is a very hard question to answer.

Actually, you might think the answer to my question is pretty obvious. Clearly, the two-year-old, five-year-old, ten-year-old, and so on in the photographs all share the *same living body*.

Of course, I don't mean that it is the *same lump of matter* each time. For the matter in Matilda's body has changed as she has become older. Each living body is composed of millions of cells, and these cells are gradually replaced.

But the same living organism continues on through all these changes. And this, you may think, is what determines the identity of a person. What makes that two-year-old, that five-year-old, that ten-year-old, and so on, all one and the same person—Matilda—is just the fact that they all share the same living body: the one she still has to this day.

But I am not so sure this "obvious" answer is correct. In fact, the imaginary case I shall now describe seems to show that it *isn't* correct.

The brain-swap case

Here are Fred and Bert.

Fred and Bert live on opposite sides of town and have never met. Fred is a five-foot-eight, slim redhead. Bert is six feet six, bald, and very fat. Bert also has a wooden leg.

One night, two Martians—Blib and Blob—break into Fred's home while he is sleeping. Blib and Blob drug Fred. Then, with their highly advanced surgical skills, they open up the top of Fred's head. Using complex scanning devices, they record precisely how Fred's brain is connected to the rest of his body. Then they remove his brain.

Blib and Blob then fly Fred's brain across town in their flying saucer. There they meet up with Flib and Flob, two other Martian scientists. Flib and Flob have been performing the exact same operation on Bert. The two teams of Martians exchange information about how the two brains were originally connected to their bodies.

Then Flib and Flob fly off to Fred's house, where they install Bert's brain in Fred's body. And Blib and Blob install Fred's brain in Bert's body.

The Martians put Fred's and Bert's skulls back together and sew up their scalps. They use a special technique to heal the scars so they can't be seen. Then they carefully remove any trace of their having been at either house.

Finally, they leave.

Morning comes. The person in Fred's bed wakes up and looks around. He doesn't know where he is. This isn't my bedroom, he thinks. He walks past a mirror and catches sight of himself. He gets a shock. He seems to have completely changed in appearance. He thought he was fat, but now he is thin. He thought he was six feet six, but now he is five feet eight. He feels sure he used to be bald, but now he has lots of bright red hair. He seems to remember having had brown eyes, but now his eyes are blue. He thought he had a wooden leg, but now he has two normal legs. What's happened to me? he asks himself.

There is a knock at the door. The person with Fred's body goes to answer it. It's the postman. "Oh, hello, Fred," says the postman. The postman thinks it is Fred because it's Fred's body that he sees in front of him. But the person with Fred's body replies, "I'm not Fred! I'm Bert! What's going on?"

Of course, the person who wakes up at Bert's house gets a similar surprise.

Where do Fred and Bert end up?

Now ask yourself: *where do Fred and Bert end up?*

When I consider this story, it seems right to say that Fred now has Bert's body, and Bert now has Fred's. Fred and Bert have *swapped bodies.* The person with Fred's body has Bert's brain, so now he has all of Bert's memories. He also has all of Bert's personality traits: he has Bert's taste for rare steak, his hatred of classical music, his short temper, his mean streak, and so on. He even *believes* he is Bert. But then surely the person with Fred's body really is Bert. Doesn't he have everything that's essential so far as being Bert is concerned?

Now let's go back to our original question: what makes this two-year-old,  this ten-year-old, this twenty-five-year-old, and this seventy-five-year-old all the same person? Our first answer was the fact that they all share the same living body—the one that Matilda still has to this day. But it now seems that *this answer cannot be right.*

What the brain swap case seems to show is that a person doesn't necessarily end up where their body ends up. In the brain-swap case, Fred doesn't end up where his body ends up. Fred ends up with Bert's body and Bert ends up with Fred's.

Of course, in the normal course of things, brain swaps never take place. People do usually end up where their bodies end up. But the brain swap case seems to show that it is at least *possible* for people to swap bodies.

So Matilda has actually ended up with the same body. But she didn't have to. If at some point her brain had been moved to a different body, then she would have ended up with that different body.

An objection

Some (though certainly not all) philosophers are convinced by such brain-swap arguments. They take them to show that having a particular body is inessential so far as personal identity is concerned.

But perhaps you are unconvinced by the argument. Perhaps you don't believe that the person with Bert's body will be Fred. Something that might cause you to object is the fact that the person with Bert's body will not be very Fred-like after all. You might argue like this: suppose Fred was a very good runner. Suppose he had won gold medals at the Olympic Games. Running was Fred's whole life.

Now the person in Fred's body finds himself with a very fat, unfit body and a wooden leg. He can't run at all. Understandably, this affects his personality greatly. Instead of being happy and outgoing, he may become very depressed, perhaps even suicidal. But then surely he isn't really Fred, for Fred is a happy and outgoing person.

I don't agree. I don't think this shows it would not be Fred who now has Bert's body. Of course, it's true that finding himself with such a different body might make Fred feel very depressed. But I think it would still be *Fred* who was depressed. Forget the brain-swap case for a moment. Suppose instead that in the normal course of things Fred loses a leg, loses his hair, and suddenly puts on 40 pounds in weight due to an illness.

This too would make him very depressed. But surely, it would still be Fred. Just because Fred becomes very depressed doesn't mean it isn't still Fred.

Of course, if this did happen to Fred, we might well say that Fred "isn't the same person anymore." We might say that he "isn't the person he used to be." But we wouldn't mean by this that the person we are now presented with is not Fred. We would just mean that he had changed a lot. Wouldn't we be admitting that it is still Fred by saying that Fred "isn't the person he used to be"?

So I have to say I don't agree with this objection. Just because the person with Bert's body feels very depressed whereas Fred previously was happy and outgoing doesn't show that it isn't Fred who now has Bert's body.

The brain-scanner case

Perhaps you still aren't convinced. You might say that the body is relevant to personal identity, but it is not the whole of the body that is relevant, just a bit of it. The relevant bit is the brain. You might agree that Fred and Bert have swapped bodies. But of course they haven't swapped brains. Fred and Bert still end up where their brains end up. So, you may say, the brain-swap case doesn't show that it isn't the brain that determines where the person ends up.

I agree that the brain-swap case doesn't show that it isn't the brain that determines where the person ends up. However, let's now change the story slightly. Suppose that the Martians *don't* swap your brains around. Rather, they use a *brain scanner* instead. The brain scanner works like this. The machine is wired up to two helmets.

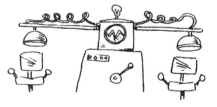

BRAIN SCANNER

When these helmets are placed on two heads, the machine records exactly how the two brains inside are wired up, how all their neurons are spliced together, how all the chemicals are balanced, and everything else. All this information is stored in the machine. Then, at the press of a button, this information is used to restructure each brain just as the other was structured.

It seems that a person's personality, memories, and other psychological attributes are fixed by how their brains are structured. So by swapping around the way the brains are structured, the brain scanner *also* swaps around all these psychological attributes.

Now suppose that, instead of swapping Fred's and Bert's brains around, Blib and Blob simply use this brain scanner. They restructure Fred's brain in the way that Bert's was structured and restructure Bert's brain in the way that Fred's was structured. Notice that the two brains stay where they are. They are simply reorganized.

By reorganizing the two brains, Blib and Blob swap the two sets of memories and personality traits. Fred's memory and personality traits move from his body over to Bert's, and Bert's move over to Fred's.

BRAIN SCANNER

After having performed this swap on an unconscious Fred and Bert, the Martians place the person with Fred's body back in Fred's bed and the person with Bert's body back in Bert's bed.

Of course, the result will be just as it was in the brain-swap case. The person who wakes up in Fred's bed the next morning will have Bert's personality and memories. So again, he will be shocked by his appearance, will think he is Bert, and so on.

Now ask yourself, where do Fred and Bert end up? Surely, Fred ends up with Bert's body, and Bert with Fred's, just as in the brain swap case. But if that is right, then *a person doesn't have to go where their brain goes*. In the normal course of things, people do end up where their brains end up. But it seems that it is at least possible for persons to swap around their entire bodies, including their brains.

In fact, what the brain-scanner case seems to show is that what determines the identity of a person is where the relevant memories and personality traits end up, not where their body or any part of it ends up.

Is a person like a rope?

We have arrived at the view that what is relevant as far as personal identity is concerned is having the right memories and personality traits. What makes the person in Fred's body Bert is that he has Bert's memories and his personality traits. It does not matter that he no longer has Bert's body.

If that is right, then what makes the two-year-old, ten-year-old, twenty-five-year-old, fifty-year-old, and seventy-five-year-old in the photographs in Matilda's album one and the same person is the fact that these individuals share the same memories and personality traits. That is what ties them all together as a single person. It may as a matter of fact be true that Matilda has one and the same living body throughout, but that is not what *makes* the two-year-old, ten-year-old, and so on, all Matilda. There is no reason in principle why Matilda should not swap bodies with someone else, just as Fred and Bert did.

Of course, in order for this seventy-five-year-old

to be the same person as this two-year-old,

they do not have to have all the same memories. That would be ridiculous. At the age of seventy, there are things Matilda remembers having done that she hasn't yet done at the age of two. There are also plenty of things she has done that she has completely forgotten about.

What seems to be important, as far as personal identity is concerned, is that there be the right sort of continuity to the memories and personality. Obviously, a person doesn't have to have exactly the same memories and exactly the same personality throughout their life. But there has at least got to be some sort of overlap.

Here is an example of such an overlap. Matilda's memory is very poor. She can remember nothing of when she was two years old or even when she was five years old. Still, she can remember something of when she was ten years old. Suppose that when she was ten years old, she could then remember being five, though she still could remember nothing of being two. And suppose that when she was five years old, she could then remember something of when she was two.

So there is an overlapping series of memories linking Matilda as she is now back to that two-year-old, despite the fact that she now has no memory of the time when she was two.

You might think of Matilda's life history as being a bit like this rope. The rope is made up of overlapping fibers, all of which are much shorter than the rope itself. Some fibers reach from the beginning to a third of the way down its length, other fibers reach from a quarter to three-quarters down its length, and still other fibers stretch only the length of the final third. None of the fibers poking out of one end of the rope can be found poking out of the other end. Still, all these fibers form a single rope because of the way the fibers overlap. Similarly, Matilda's memories and personality traits now are quite different from those she had as a two-year-old. Still, this two-year-old and this seventy-five-year-old are both Matilda because there is an overlapping series of memories and personality traits linking them together.

Reincarnation

If what makes a person you is your possessing the right personality and memories, whether or not you have the same physical body, then it seems that when you die, you might come back later with a different body. Perhaps this never actually happens. The point is that it could happen.

To come back to life with a new body is to be reincarnated. Some religions claim that we are all reincarnated.

One way in which you might be reincarnated is if we used the brain scanner I talked about earlier to scan your brain shortly before you died, then later on used it to restructure someone else's brain so that your memories and personality traits were transferred over to the other person's body. It seems you would be brought back to life with a different body.

So science may one day allow us to be reincarnated. Of course, it would hardly be fair for you to take over the body of another person, for what would happen to that person. But perhaps a new body might be made for you, either by cloning or by some other process. Then you might live for centuries. When your old body wore out, you could change it for a new one, much as you might change an old, broken-down car for a new one.

The soul

Some people, especially religious people, believe that each of us has a *soul*. A soul is a very peculiar sort of thing. We aren't talking about a physical thing made out of physical stuff. We are talking about something *nonphysical*. Indeed, a soul is a supernatural thing —the thing which many believe goes up to heaven when our physical body dies.

Now, your soul, if you have one, is apparently connected to your physical body. It controls your physical body. But it can be separated from your body. In fact, your soul can exist without any physical body at all.

Of course, if each person is really a soul, then it would be possible in principle for people to swap bodies. Your soul could come to be connected to a different physical body instead.

However, it's important to realize that, by suggesting that you might swap bodies with someone, I'm certainly not suggesting you have a soul. Certainly, if we have souls, then body swaps are possible. But it does not follow that if body swaps are possible, then we have souls.

I'm suggesting that all that's required for persons to swap bodies is that certain psychological properties (such as being bad-tempered or being able to remember the war) be switched from one body to the other. You don't have to move any physical part of one body over to the other, not even the brain. But neither do you have to move some sort of nonphysical, supernatural, soul-stuff thing over from one body to the other.

In fact, as I will now explain, even if someone else has your soul, that doesn't make them you.

The soul-swap case

Suppose that you and I each have a soul, and that these two souls will swap in two minutes. However, everything else—including all our memories and psychological traits—will remain in place. My soul will come to have your body, memories, and personality traits. Your soul will come to have mine.

Notice that after the swap, everything will seem exactly the same, not only to everyone else but also to the two of us (wherever we end up). The person who ends up with this body will have the memories and personality that go with this body. So even if you end up with this body, you won't remember any swap. You won't remember any of your own past, only mine.

Suppose this soul swap happens. Where do you and I end up? If we say that the person is the soul, and goes wherever their soul goes, then we must say that the person with my soul but your body, memories, and personality traits is now me. And the person with your soul but my body, memories, and personality traits is now you.

But this can't be right, can it? Surely, the person with your body won't be me, despite the fact you now have my soul. Because you are nothing like me. You have none of my memories. Your personality is quite different from mine. When asked who you are, you give my name. If asked about your relatives, you talk about my relatives. It certainly won't be easy to convince you that you are not who you think you are.

In fact, this sort of soul swap could be happening all the time and no one, including the people involved, would be any the wiser. Perhaps your soul and mine did just swap five minutes ago. What difference would it make? No one would notice. Not even us!

Isn't it more plausible to say that, even if there are such things as souls, it is the person with all your memories and personality traits that is you, no matter whose soul he or she might happen to have? In that case, it seems that not only is the body irrelevant as far as our question about personal identity is concerned, so, too, is the soul.

Three theories

We have now looked at three different theories about personal identity.

The first theory we looked at holds that the living body determines the identity of a person. By this theory, people end up where their bodies end up. Let's call this theory the *Body Theory* of personal identity. The brain-scanner case seems to show that the Body Theory is wrong: it is possible for people to swap bodies.

We also looked at the theory that each person has an immaterial soul and that this is what determines their identity. By this theory, people end up wherever their souls end up. Let's call this the *Soul Theory* of personal identity. It seems that, even if there are such things as souls, it would be possible for persons to swap souls, which means that the Soul Theory cannot be right, either.

So far, the theory that seems most plausible is the theory that memory and personality traits determine personal identity. Let's call this the *Stream Theory* of personal identity. By the Stream Theory, what links together the two-year-old, five-year-old, ten-year-old, and so on that appear in Matilda's photo album as a single person is the fact that they share a stream of memories and personality traits. They are psychologically continuous with one another. If this psychological stream were to pass from one body to another, or even from one soul to another (if there are such things), then so, too, would Matilda.

The Mars "Transporter" Case and the Two-of-You Problem

I have tried to make the Stream Theory seem as plausible as possible. But I must now reveal that there is a serious problem with it. I shall call this problem the Two-of-You Problem.

In order to help explain the Two-of-You Problem, let's take a look at an example I call the Mars "Transporter" Case.

Suppose Martian scientists developed a machine that could scan a human body (or any physical object, for that matter) and then produce a copy that is indistinguishable down to the last atom. You are presented with this machine. You are asked to step into a cubicle and press the red button to start the machine. You do so. There is a zap. Your original body is instantaneously vaporized. But just before it is destroyed, it is scanned and all the information needed to produce a duplicate body is transmitted to Mars where there is a similar machine. The machine on Mars then produces a duplicate body. This all takes but a second or two.

Of course, the person who steps out of the cubicle on Mars is not only physically just like you. He (or she) is also psychologically continuous with you. He has all of your personality traits. He has all of your memories. When asked who he is, he gives your name. He seems to remember having just stepped into the machine on Earth and pressed the red button.

Now, if we accept the Stream Theory of personal identity, then we must say that the person on Mars *really is you*. For that person is

psychologically continuous with you. What we have here really is a *transporter*. The machine can transport people from Earth to Mars, and back again if they so wish. Perhaps you find this plausible. Perhaps you would be happy to step into the machine and press the red button, thinking that you will be whizzed off to Mars.

But I'm not so sure. Suppose we change the story slightly. Suppose that instead of producing *one* duplicate body on Mars, we program the machine to produce *two*. Two people get out of the cubicle on Mars, both of whom are psychologically continuous with you. One might say that in this case the psychological stream divides. It branches into two.

This story lands the Stream Theory in deep trouble, because it says since both people are psychologically continuous with you, both people *are* you. Both are one and the same person as you. But they *can't* both be one and the same person as you, for it would then follow that they are one and the same person as each other, which clearly they are not: there are *two* of them, not one. They may be *exactly similar*, but they are not *one and the same person*. So it seems the psychological Stream Theory can't be correct.

The Single Stream Theory

We have seen that the possibility of the psychological stream dividing raises a big problem for the Stream Theory. Can the theory be altered to deal with this problem?

Some philosophers have suggested that we only need to add on a further condition to solve the problem. The condition requires that there be *no dividing of the psychological stream*. It says that if at some point the psychological stream does branch into two, then *neither* of the later individuals is identical with the earlier one. At the moment the stream divides, two new people come into existence, and the original person is no more. However, if there is no dividing of the stream—if there is only one later individual psychologically continuous with the earlier individual—then the later and earlier individuals are one and the same person.

Let's call this the *Single Stream Theory* of personal identity.

The duplicator gun

One problem the Single Stream Theory has to deal with can be brought out by two more thought experiments.

Suppose that Martian scientists develop a scanning machine that can scan bodies from a great distance and then duplicate them. Let's call it the *duplicator gun*. I leave my front door and start to walk down the street. Unknown to me, the Martians, who are flying out in space, then aim the duplicator gun at me and press the starting button. The machine instantly reads off exactly how I am physically put together and produces an atom-for-atom duplicate of me in a cubicle on board their spacecraft. Of course, the duplicate that steps out of the cubicle on the spacecraft is psychologically continuous with me. It seems to him just as if he stepped out of my front door and started walking down the street when suddenly the street turned into a Martian spacecraft. Back on Earth, the person with my original body reaches the end of the street and turns the corner. He is oblivious of what has happened.

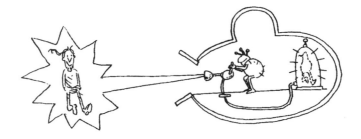

In this story, my psychological stream branches into two. There are now two individuals who are psychologically just like the earlier me: the individual who reaches the end of the street and turns the corner; and the individual who steps out of the cubicle on the spacecraft. So where am I? According to the Single Stream Theory, *neither* of these two individuals is me. As the duplicating gun is fired, the original me disappears and two new people come into existence. Neither the person who steps out of the cubicle on the spacecraft *nor the person who reaches the end of the street* is Stephen Law. Stephen Law has *ceased to exist.*

But isn't this absurd? How can the Martians make me cease to exist just by producing a copy of me? Whether or not the Martians make a copy of me as I walk down the street, it's still me who reaches the end of the street and turns the corner, right? But that is just what the Single Stream Theory contradicts. So it seems the Single Stream Theory must be wrong.

Here is another difficult case for the Single Stream Theory. Suppose that no one reaches the end of the street to turn the corner. The Martians fire the duplicator gun and produce a copy just as before, only this time, just as the duplicate starts to materialize, I step off the curb and a passing truck squashes my body flat (I forgot to look).

Where am I now? Do I still exist? According to the Single Stream Theory, I do still exist. In fact, I am *transported to the spacecraft*. In this story, exactly one later individual is psychologically continuous with the earlier me: the person who steps out of the cubicle on board the spacecraft. Therefore, according to the Single Stream Theory, the person on board the spacecraft is me.

But again, isn't this absurd? Surely I am *dead*. The fact that the Martians happened to make an exact copy of me the instant before my body is flattened by the truck doesn't alter this fact. There may be a person *just like me* on the spacecraft. But that person isn't actually me.

So the Single Stream Theory runs into problems because it has some rather absurd-sounding consequences. Perhaps these problems can be dealt with.

But perhaps they can't be dealt with. Perhaps what these last two science fiction cases involving the duplicator gun show is that having a certain living body is not irrelevant as far as personal identity is concerned. Perhaps we were too easily persuaded by the brain-swap and brain-scanner cases. Regarding the first story about the duplicator gun, doesn't it seem right to say that the person who reaches the end of the street is me because he is the same living organism that left my house? It does not matter that a copy of that living organism has been produced elsewhere. In the second story about the duplicator gun, doesn't it sound right to say that the person on the spacecraft isn't me because he is not the one and the same living organism as left my house? Unfortunately, that living organism is no more: it was flattened by a truck.

So we are presented with two conflicting sets of intuitions. On the one hand, our intuitions about the brain-swap case and brain-scanner case tell us that having a certain living body is completely irrelevant as far as personal identity is concerned. On the other hand, our intuitions about the two stories involving the duplicator gun suggest that having a certain living body is very relevant as far as personal identity is concerned. Which of these conflicting sets of intuitions are we to trust? I must admit: I am very confused.

The issues we have been discussing are brought out in my last science-fiction story, set out below. The story ends with my facing a terrible dilemma. I will leave it up to you to decide what I should do.

Vacation of a lifetime?

Blib and Blob come to visit me one day. They set up their Martian "transporter" (which we talked about earlier) in my front room, and explain to me how it works. They demonstrate by using it to "transport" Blib from a cubicle on one side of the room to one on the other side of the room and back again. "See!" says Blib. "It's completely reliable!"

Blib and Blob explain that they have set up similar cubicles all over the universe at their favorite vacation destinations, and they offer to let me use them to tour the universe. I need only step into the cubicle in front of me, dial in my first destination, and press the red button.

What an incredible opportunity, I think. I step in, dial in my chosen destination (I decide to visit a spaceship hovering over the rings of Saturn), and press the button. From there I spend months traveling to all sorts of exotic places. I have the time of my life.

But one day, while I am sitting on a beach on a beautiful

deserted planet way over on the far side of the galaxy, I start to think more carefully about the Martian "transporter."

A nagging doubt starts to eat at me. I'm not so sure I want to step back inside the cubicle from which I emerged a few hours ago, select a destination, and press the red button again. Actually, I'm not so sure it really was a transporter after all. Blib and Blob might have convinced themselves that it was a transporter. But perhaps they have fooled themselves. Maybe, every time someone steps inside and presses the button, that person is instantly vaporized. The organism that is produced elsewhere is just a copy of the original.

And then a horrible thought strikes me. If that is true, then *Stephen Law died months ago.* He killed himself when he stepped into the first cubicle and pressed the button. I am not Stephen Law (though I thought I was). I am merely someone *just like* Stephen Law. In fact, I have only been in existence for a few hours: the few hours since I stepped out of that cubicle over there.

So what should I do? Should I remain here alone, stranded forever on the far side of the galaxy? Or should I step into the cubicle, dial in home, and press that red button? If I do, will the person who steps out of the cubicle on Earth really be me? Or will he merely be a copy? Will I return home? Or will I die? What do you think?

Question 3

How do I know the world isn't virtual?

Jim's game

Here's Jim.

Jim is playing a computer game. The game is called Dungeons and Monsters. To win the game you have to run around inside a maze of dungeons, kill all the monsters, and collect all the treasure. As you can see, Jim loves the game. Especially killing the monsters.

I had better warn you now: something nasty happens to Jim. But we'll come to that later. First, I need to explain about *virtual reality*.

Virtual reality

The dungeons, guns, monsters, and treasure in Jim's game aren't real, of course. They form what is known as a *virtual reality*: a world created by a computer. A virtual reality is made up of a *virtual environment* where *virtual objects* can be found. In Jim's game, the dungeons and corridors are the virtual environment. The guns, monsters, and treasure are virtual objects.

You will probably have come across a virtual reality yourself.

Perhaps you have played a computer game in which you drive a car round a racetrack or fly a plane through the sky. The cars, racetrack, and planes that you see in these games are all virtual. They don't actually exist.

Wearing a virtual reality helmet

Usually, when you play one of these games, you watch the action on a sort of TV screen. But there are now other ways of experiencing virtual reality.

In fact, computer scientists have developed virtual reality *helmets*.

Here's how a virtual reality helmet works. When you put it on, you see a small screen. This screen shows the virtual environment. And the important thing about the screen is that, when you move your head about, what you see changes just as it would if you really were in such an environment. For example, if you turn your head to the left, you see what's to the left of you in the virtual environment. Look down and you see what's on the floor of the virtual environment. Spin around and you see what's behind you, and so on.

The helmet also contains little loudspeakers—one for each ear— so that you can hear what is going on inside the virtual reality. Again, these speakers change what you hear depending on which way you are facing. So, with the virtual reality helmet on, it looks and sounds as if the virtual environment is actually all around you.

Virtual hands and legs

It's also possible to reach out and pick up virtual objects. Electronic gloves have been developed that control virtual hands. Put the gloves on, and you can move the virtual hands that you see in front of you when you wear the virtual reality helmet. With these virtual hands you can steer a virtual car or fire a virtual laser gun at a virtual alien.

VIRTUAL REALITY   ACTUAL REALITY

In fact, you can even walk around inside virtual reality. The computer that generates the virtual reality can be wired up to special sensors strapped to your legs and feet. Walk forward and the computer detects this and changes what you see and hear: it makes it seem as if you are walking forward into the virtual environment.

Suppose we give Jim one of these virtual reality outfits—the helmet, gloves, and leg sensors—and connect it up to a powerful computer running a version of his favorite Dungeons and Monsters game. Then Jim can play his game, only this time it will seem much more real to him. This time it will seem to Jim as if the virtual dungeon is actually all around him. This time it will seem as if he can actually reach out and touch the walls of the dungeon with his hand.

Artificial eyes

Let's now look at a different sort of technology: artificial eyes. Unlike virtual reality, this technological breakthrough hasn't happened yet. But there seems to be no reason why it couldn't happen.

Put your hand up in front of your face and take a good look at it.

What happens when you see your hand?

First of all, light is reflected off your hand into your eyes. A lens at the front of the eye focuses this light onto a surface at the back of the eye, producing an image. Now, this surface at the back of your eye is made up of many millions of light-sensitive cells. And when light falls onto one of these cells, it produces a tiny electrical impulse. The pattern of electrical impulses sent by your hand's image then passes along a bundle of nerves (called the optic nerve) that runs from your eye into your brain. That's how you come to see your hand.

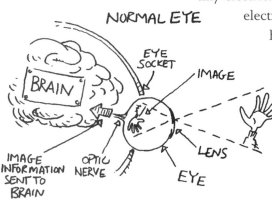

NORMAL EYE

BRAIN

EYE SOCKET

IMAGE

LENS

EYE

IMAGE INFORMATION SENT TO BRAIN

OPTIC NERVE

But does it have to be a normal human eye that sends the electrical impulses down your optic nerve and into your brain? I don't see why. Why couldn't your normal human eyes be replaced with little TV cameras instead?

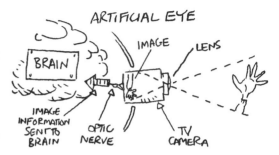

These cameras could do the job that your human eyes do now, sending down your optic nerves just the same patterns of electrical stimulation that your normal eyes send now. So everything would look just the same to you. The world seen through artificial eyes would look just like it does through normal eyes.

Having an eye on the end of a stick

In fact, in some ways having little TV-camera eyes could be a big advantage. Suppose you had artificial eyes. They could be attached to your optic nerves with extra-long cables. Then you could take out an eye and hold it in your hand. You could stick it around the back of your head—very useful if you wanted to know whether someone was following you.

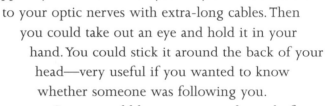

Or you could have an eye on the end of a stick—invaluable for finding that coin you dropped under the sofa.

A robot body

Scientists may one day develop not only
artificial eyes but also artificial ears:
little electronic microphones that take
the place of normal human ears.
These microphones would stimulate
the nerves that connect our normal
ears to our brains in just the way our
normal ears do.

So the ringing of a church bell would
sound just the same to someone fitted
with artificial ears.

In fact, when you think about it, there seems no reason in
principle why your *whole body* should not be replaced with an
artificial one. You could have a robot body. Here's how.

Your brain is connected to the rest of your body by a system of
nerves. Some of these nerve pathways *send out* electrical impulses.
Others *receive* electrical impulses.

Those nerves that *send out* electrical impulses send many of them
out to the muscles that enable you to move your body around. For
example, when you go to turn this page, your hand
moves because your brain sends out
a pattern of electrical impulses to certain
muscles in your arm.

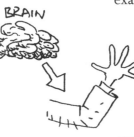

The impulses make the muscles
move. And the movement of those
muscles enables you to
move your hand. The
nerve pathways that receive electrical
impulses receive many of them from
your five senses: your ears, eyes, nose,
tongue, and skin.

That's what allows you to experience the world around you.

But now suppose this happens: your brain is removed from your old human body and fitted into a new robot body.

Then your old human body is destroyed. But that doesn't matter because your new robot body keeps your brain alive. It also stimulates the nerves running into your brain in just the way they used to be stimulated by your old human body. So your new robot body gives you experiences just like those your old human body gave you. With your new robot body you can enjoy chocolate ice cream, listen to music, smell the flowers. Everything seems just the same.

And the patterns of electrical impulses coming out of your brain make your new robot body move around in just the way your normal body did (only now they don't move muscles: they move little electric motors instead). So you can talk and walk just as before.

Surviving the death of your human body

Of course, we can't build ourselves robot bodies just yet. Technology hasn't developed that far. But it certainly seems possible that robot bodies might one day be built, perhaps in a few hundred years' time.

If robot bodies are built, we will be able to survive the death of our normal flesh-and-blood bodies. Suppose your human body accidentally got flattened by a truck. Your brain could be taken out and put in a new robot body instead.

Then you could carry on living, even though your flesh-and-blood body was dead. You would now be part human, part machine.

Robot bodies could probably also be made stronger, more durable, and in various other ways better than our ordinary flesh-and-blood bodies. You could have superhuman strength. You could be given incredibly sensitive hearing. You could even have X-ray vision.

Perhaps one day, maybe in a thousand years' time, we will *all* be robot superbeings.

Perhaps the only human parts of us left will be our brains.

Having a virtual body

It seems that not only is it possible to have a robot body, it's also possible to have a *virtual body*.

Suppose this happens. A little electrical socket is wired into the back of your neck. This socket is connected up to where the nerves running in and out of your brain join up to the rest of your body. The socket allows you to connect your brain up to an incredibly powerful supercomputer. You only need to plug a cable connected to the computer into your socket and flip a little switch attached to the back of your neck.

When you flip the switch, all of the electrical impulses coming out of your brain that would go on to move your body about are diverted. They are sent off to the supercomputer instead. And rather than receiving electrical impulses from your eyes, ears, nose, tongue, and skin, your brain receives them from the supercomputer.

Now, suppose this computer is running a virtual reality program. Here's how it would work: You lie down on a bed next to the computer and plug yourself in. Then you reach around to the back of your neck and flip that switch. Of course, the moment you flip the switch, your body goes limp: you've just disconnected your body from your brain.

But that's not how it seems to you. It seems to you that you can still move your body. Suppose you try to wiggle your fingers in front of your face. The computer registers the finger-wiggling electrical impulses coming out of your brain. It then sends back to your brain just the sort of impulses it would receive from your eyes and hands if you really were wiggling your fingers in front of your face. So this is what you see. It looks and feels to you just as if you were wiggling your fingers in front of your face. But of course, the fingers you now see wiggling are *virtual* fingers, not real fingers. Your real hands lie quite still on the bed.

In fact, if the computer were powerful enough, it could generate a *whole virtual environment* for you. For example, it could make it seem to you as if you were lying in the woods inhabited by fabulous singing birds and beautiful flowers. You could get up and walk about in the woods. The trees you saw, the birds you heard, and the flowers you smelled would not be real, of course. They would all be virtual. And the body it seemed that you now had would be a virtual body, not a real one. Your real body would still be lying motionless on the bed.

Switching over to a virtual body might be a pleasant way to spend an evening. After a hard day at work you could relax by switching to a virtual body and exploring a virtual environment. You could invent whatever strange new world you felt like occupying for a few hours.

You could even choose what your virtual body looked like. For example, you could choose to look like Elvis Presley and visit a planet made entirely out of marshmallows.

Having seen how you might come to have a virtual body in a virtual environment, let's take a break. I shall now tell you what happens to Jim.

Intermission: a horror story

One day, two Martians—Blib and Blob—arrive on Earth. Blib and Blob are here to study human beings. They decide to make Jim their first subject and set about secretly observing his behavior.

Blib and Blob are fascinated to see just how much Jim loves his computer game Dungeons and Monsters. They observe that Jim devotes every spare minute of his time to playing the game. Jim's father cooks Jim's dinner. "Come and get it, Jim!" he shouts up the stairs. The Martians notice that Jim has to be asked six times. They also notice that, after Jim has gulped down his food, he always runs straight back upstairs and starts playing the game again.

Blib and Blob also observe that every time a new version of the Dungeons and Monsters game is brought out, Jim is desperate to get a hold of a copy. For the two months before Christmas, Jim's every other sentence is: "Mom, Dad, *please* can I have the new Dungeons and Monsters game for Christmas?"

After making all these observations, Blib and Blob decide that what would make Jim happiest would be if he could be left permanently to play the most realistic version of Dungeons and Monsters imaginable And so they decide to make Jim happy.

It is Christmas morning. Jim begins to wake. The first thing he notices is his bed. It feels hard and cold, like stone. And it smells kind of strange, too. Sort of dank and musty. Like mushrooms. And he can hear a dripping noise.

Jim slowly opens his eyes. He finds himself in a long, stone corridor. The corridor is lit by torches hanging from rusty metal brackets. There are passages off left and right. Jim turns to look behind him. He sees that the corridor stretches back into the shadows in just the same way.

This corridor seems vaguely familiar to Jim. Then he remembers: it looks just like the one in Dungeons and Monsters. Only this corridor seems real. He can reach out and run his fingers down the cold, slimy walls.

Then Jim's blood runs cold, because he hears a howl. It is a howl Jim has heard a thousand times before. Only this time the howl doesn't come out of the little loudspeakers next to his computer. This time the howl comes from out of the shadows at the end of the corridor. This time the howl is real. And so, too, are those shuffling footsteps. Jim knows what's coming. With his heart pounding in his ears, Jim staggers to his feet. He starts to run.

Jim's parents are puzzled. They have bought Jim a new computer program with the very latest Dungeons and Monsters game. So why hasn't he rushed downstairs to open his present as usual? His parents climb the stairs and slowly open his bedroom door. They peek inside.

"Jim? Are you awake?" The room is quiet. The curtains are still drawn. And Jim's bed is empty.

The bedroom is lit by an eerie light. Jim's parents turn to see that the light is coming from a computer screen down on the floor. But it is not Jim's own computer they are looking at. As their eyes begin to adjust to the darkness, they can just make out that the flickering screen is attached to a large gray box.

In fact, this gray box is a Martian supercomputer. Blib and Blob have been busy. They built this computer to run the most realistic version of Dungeons and Monsters you could possibly imagine. They built the computer especially for Jim.

"AAARGH!!!" Jim's parents scream in horror. As the image on the screen flickers more brightly for an instant, filling the room with light, they see that there in the shadows behind the computer is a *human brain floating in a glass vat.*

It is Jim's living brain. And it is fully conscious. Blib and Blob have come in the night and removed Jim's brain. They have destroyed the rest of Jim's body and placed his brain in this life-supporting vat of liquid. Then they connected his brain up to their computer. Jim now has a virtual body in a virtual environment: the environment of Dungeons and Monsters. Jim is now playing the most realistic version of Dungeons and Monsters imaginable. Only he can't stop. And he can't tell it's not real.

Jim's parents' eyes turn to the image on the computer screen. It's Jim! They see him being chased down a narrow corridor by a huge monster. "My poor Jim!" cries his mother. But of course it is quite pointless to shout. All Jim can hear is the howling monster hot on his heels. Jim will never hear his mother's voice again.

In shock, Jim's parents watch as he tries to shake off the monster. Eventually, he makes a desperate lunge into some shadows. He crouches motionless, daring not even to breathe. The monster stops. It sniffs briefly at the damp air. And then it is gone. For now.

Jim's parents can bear to watch no longer. They turn away from the screen. Only then do they notice that a card has been left tied to the computer with a red ribbon. Trembling, they move closer. Finally, in the flickering glow from the screen, they make out the message written on the card in a strange, spidery scrawl. The message reads:

Are YOU a brain in a vat?

A pretty ghastly story, don't you agree? Jim ends up trapped inside a horrible virtual reality so lifelike that he can't tell it's not real. And the Martians thought they were doing him a favor.

Stories about brains in vats are very interesting to philosophers. They are particularly interesting to those philosophers who are interested in the question: *what, if anything, can we know about the world around us?* This is the question we are now going to look at.

Here's a slightly different brain-in-a-vat story—a story about you. Suppose that last night Blib and Blob came to your house while you were sleeping. They drugged you and whisked you off to Mars in their flying saucer. They removed your brain from your body, floated it in a glass vat of life-supporting fluid, and connected it up to a supercomputer.

Your body was then destroyed.

It is the supercomputer that now controls all your experiences. Snap your fingers. When you go to snap your fingers, the computer monitors the impulses leaving your brain: the impulses that would have gone on to move your fingers if you still had some. The computer then stimulates the nerve endings that used to be connected to your eyes, fingertips, ears, and so on, so that it seems to you that you see, feel, and hear your fingers move and hear the snap. But in fact you don't have real fingers anymore. You have only virtual computer-generated fingers.

The computer that creates these experiences is incredibly advanced. It copies your normal environment down to the very last detail. So everything seems to you just as it would if what you were experiencing were real. Your virtual bedroom seems exactly like your real bedroom. Your virtual parents act just like your real parents.

VIRTUAL PARENTS   REAL PARENTS

Your virtual street seems just like your real street.

Now the big philosophical question this story raises is *how do you know you're not a brain in a vat?* How do you know the world you see around you isn't virtual? Perhaps Martians really *did* come last night. Perhaps they really *did* take out your brain and connect it to a super-computer. If they did, could you tell? No. It seems not, because everything would now seem exactly the same to you.

Perhaps you've ALWAYS been a brain in a vat

Here's an even more frightening thought. Perhaps you have *always* been a brain in a vat, right from birth. Perhaps planet Earth doesn't exist. Perhaps the things with which you seem so familiar—your house, your neighborhood, your friends and family—are no more "real" than the places and characters in Jim's Dungeons and Monsters game. Perhaps they were made up by Martian computer programmers. Perhaps these Martians are studying your brain right now to see how it reacts to the world that they have invented.

In other words, perhaps the only reality you have ever known is a virtual reality. Could you tell? No. It seems not.

How do you know you're not a brain in a vat?

Now, of course you don't really believe you're a brain in a vat. In fact, like me, you believe you're *not* a brain in a vat. But the question is: do you *know* that you're not a brain in a vat? Do you know that the world you seem to see around you is real?

The answer seems to be: no, you don't *know*. You may believe the world you see is real. And perhaps it is true that the world you see is real. But even if it is true, it seems you don't *know* that it's real. In order to know something, you surely need some *reason* to believe that it is true. And you have no reason at all to believe that it is a real world that you see and not a virtual one, because *everything would seem exactly the same to you even if it were virtual*. So, amazingly, it seems you don't know you're not a brain in a vat!

In fact, it seems you don't know *anything* about the world out there. For all you know, the hands you see in front of you, this book you seem to hold in your hands, that tree you seem to see outside your window, even planet Earth could all be virtual.

What is skepticism?

The argument that we have just looked at—the argument that you don't know anything about the world around you—is called a *skeptical* argument. Skeptics claim that we don't really know what we think we know. The claim that you don't know anything of the world about you is called *skepticism about the external world*.

Skepticism against common sense

Of course, the common sense view is that we do know about the external world. In fact, if you were to say, "I don't know that trees exist," especially while looking at a tree in broad daylight, other people would think you had gone mad.

But according to the skeptic, you would be quite right. You *don't* know that trees exist. Common sense is wrong.

Other examples of common sense being wrong

The skeptic's argument can make some people quite angry. The existence of trees is one of our most basic beliefs—as I say, we feel it's just common sense. There are many beliefs that we would be quite happy to give up were someone to show us we must be wrong. But when it comes to our most basic common sense beliefs—such as the belief that we know that trees exist—we are not at all happy about giving them up.

Having our most basic beliefs challenged can be a very uncomfortable experience, especially when we can't see how to defend them. So some people get very angry. They say that the philosopher is talking complete nonsense. "That's just plain *stupid!*" they shout. "Of *course*, I know that trees exist." And they walk off in a huff.

But the philosopher can point out that there are many other cases where common sense has turned out to be wrong. For example, it was once the common sense view that the earth is flat. People thought it was obvious that the earth is flat. After all, it looks flat, doesn't it? Sailors even used to worry about sailing over the edge.

Now, some people got very angry when this common sense belief of theirs was challenged: "Don't be ridiculous!" they shouted. "Of course the earth is flat!" And they stomped off.

But we now know that the earth isn't flat. Common sense was wrong.

Here's another example of how common sense can be wrong. Take a look at this sheet of paper. It has two sides: this side . . .

. . . and this side. Now ask yourself: could there be a piece of paper that had only *one side*? Most people would say, "Of course not. Any sheet of paper just *has* to have two sides. That's just common sense."

But actually common sense is wrong about this. If you take a strip of paper like this:

. . . give it a half twist . . .

. . . and then join the two ends together to form a loop . . .

. . . you will find that you now have a piece of paper with *only one* side. The strip (called a Möbius strip) *looks* like it still has two sides, but when you pick one side and follow it around the loop, you find that what look like two different sides are actually the same side.

So common sense has turned out to be wrong about many things. Perhaps common sense is also wrong about our knowing that trees exist.

What the skeptic ISN'T claiming

It is worth getting clear what our skeptic isn't claiming, so we don't get confused.

First, the skeptic isn't claiming to know that you or they are a brain in a vat. They are claiming only that *no one can know one way or the other* whether or not they or anyone else is a brain in a vat.

Second, they are not just claiming that you cannot be *absolutely certain* that the world you see is real and not virtual. They are claiming much more than that. They are claiming that you have *no reason at all* to believe that it is a real world you see, not a virtual one.

Third, they are not going so far as to claim that no one can know *anything at all*. After all, they are themselves claiming to know *something*: that no one can know about the external world.

An ancient puzzle

So we are faced with a difficult puzzle. On the one hand, the common sense view is that we do know that trees exist. We really don't want to give up this common view (actually, I'm not sure we could give it up, even if we wanted to). On the other hand, the skeptic has an argument which seems to show that the common sense view is wrong: we don't know that trees exist. Which view is correct?

Although I have dressed it up in modern clothing, this puzzle is actually very old. In fact, it is one of the best-known philosophical puzzles. Even today, at universities all over the world, philosophers are working on this puzzle. And they still aren't agreed about whether the skeptic is right. I must admit: I just don't know whether or not the skeptic is right.

Down through the centuries many philosophers have tried to deal with skepticism. They have tried to show that common sense is right: we do know about the world out there after all. Some of their attempts at defeating the skeptic are very clever. But do any of them actually work? Let's now take a look at one of these attempts.

Ockham's razor

The skeptic presents us with two theories or hypotheses. The first hypothesis—the common sense hypothesis—is that you are not a brain in a vat: the world you see around you is real. The second hypothesis is that you are a brain in a vat: the world you see is merely virtual.

The skeptic says that you have no more reason to believe the first hypothesis than you do to believe the second. Both hypotheses are equally well supported by the evidence of your senses. Everything would seem just the same to you either way. So you don't know that the first hypothesis is true and the second false.

Now, we may agree with the skeptic that how things seem to you is *consistent* with both hypotheses. But, as I explain below, it doesn't follow from this that how things seem equally *supports* both hypotheses.

There is a famous philosophical principle which says that when you are presented with two hypotheses, both of which are otherwise equally supported by the evidence, it is always reasonable to believe the *simpler* hypothesis. This principle is called *Ockham's razor*. It seems a very plausible principle.

The two boxes example

Here's an illustration of how Ockham's
razor works. Suppose you are shown
a box with a button on the side and
a lightbulb on top. You see that,
whenever the button is pressed, the
light comes on. Otherwise the light
stays off.

Now let's look at two competing
hypotheses, both of which explain what you see.

The first hypothesis is that the button and bulb are linked by a
circuit to a battery inside the box. Press the button and the circuit
is completed. That lights up the bulb.

The second hypothesis is more complicated. It says that the
button is attached to an electrical circuit linking a battery to a
second lightbulb inside the box. When the button is pressed, this
interior lightbulb comes on. A light sensor inside the box then
detects this and connects a second electrical circuit linking a *second*
battery to the bulb you see on the outside of the box. That lights
up the outside bulb.

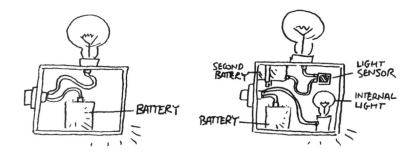

Now, which of these two hypotheses is more reasonable, do you
think? True, both hypotheses are equally *consistent* with what you
have seen: with both hypotheses, the light will come on when and
only when you press the button. But it seems wrong to say that

both hypotheses are equally *reasonable*. Surely it is more reasonable to believe the first hypothesis than it is to believe the second, because the second hypothesis is *less simple*: it says there are two electrical circuits in the box, not one.

Can we use Ockham's razor to defeat the skeptic? Perhaps. You might say that of our two hypotheses—the hypothesis that it is a real world that you see and the hypothesis that it is merely virtual —the first hypothesis is simpler. Because while the first hypothesis says there's just *one* world, the second hypothesis in effect says there are *two*: there's an actual world filled with Martians, a supercomputer, a vat, and your brain, within which is created a second virtual world containing virtual trees, houses, people, and so on. So, given that the first hypothesis is simpler, that means it's more reasonable.

Therefore, the skeptic is wrong: it is more reasonable to believe it is a real world that you see, not a virtual world, despite the fact that how things seem to you is equally consistent with both hypotheses.

A worry

What do you think about this reply to the skeptic's argument? I certainly have some worries about it. One worry I have is this: is the hypothesis that it is a real world you see really the simpler hypothesis? That rather depends on what is meant by "simpler." In fact, while there are ways in which the first hypothesis is simpler, there are also ways in which it's less simple.

For example, someone might say that the second hypothesis is simpler because it needs *far fewer real physical objects*: just the Martians, your brain in a vat, and a supercomputer. There is no need to suppose that planet Earth with all its trees, houses, cats, dogs, mountains, cars, and so on also really exists.

Or someone might say that the second hypothesis is simpler because it needs *far fewer real minds*. If your friends, family, neighbors, and so on are merely virtual, then so, too, are their minds. The only real minds the second hypothesis needs are your mind plus those of the computer operators.

So, it isn't obvious that the first hypothesis really is simpler. In fact, you might argue that it is actually the second hypothesis that is simpler and therefore more reasonable. It's actually more reasonable to believe you are a brain in a vat!

Am I an island?

If the skeptics are right (and I'm not saying they *are* right), then each of us is in an important way detached from the world around us. You know nothing about the world out there. You have no reason at all to believe that you inhabit a world of trees, houses, cats, dogs, mountains, and cars. And you have no reason at all to think that you are surrounded by other people. For all you know, your entire world—including all the people in it (including even me)—is merely virtual.

That is quite a scary thought. It forces you to think of yourself in a very different way. Someone once said, "No man is an island." But if the skeptic is right, there is a sense in which this is false. Each of us is stranded on our own desert island, unable to know anything of the world that lies beyond the horizon of our own sensory experiences. We are closed off from the world beyond. And we are closed off from one another. We are prisoners within our own minds.

The skeptic paints a very lonely picture.

Yet in another way skepticism makes no difference at all. Skepticism leaves our day-to-day lives untouched. Even the skeptics continue with their daily routine. They feed the cat. They do the dishes. They go off to work. They meet a friend for coffee. Not even the skeptics can really stop themselves believing that the world they see is real, despite the fact that they believe they have no reason to believe it's real. It seems we are natural-born believers: we just can't help ourselves.

But is the skeptic right? I'm just not sure. What do you think?

Question 4

Should I eat meat?

The story of Errol, the explorer
Errol was an explorer. He loved to sail
the seas looking for new lands.

   On one of his trips up to the north,
not far from where the ice begins, Errol
discovered a small, mountainous island
covered in forest. He decided to leave
his crew behind on the ship and to go ashore in a rowing boat,
quite alone.

   Errol took with him some supplies: lemonade and sandwiches.
That night he slept beside the sea in a hammock suspended
between two large pine trees.

   The next day, Errol started to walk into the forest. After an hour
or so, he began to see signs of human life. There were clearings in
the forest and burnt areas that looked like they had once been
campfires. This made Errol very excited. He thought he was about
to discover a new tribe.

Eventually, after several hours, Errol came to a
larger clearing. And there, in the middle of the
clearing, were three strangely dressed people.

The three strangers wore purple vests and odd red hats shaped like
upside-down triangles. They stood in silence, looking him up and
down. It seemed as if they had been waiting for him.

Errol raised his hand as a sign of friendship. At this, the three
strangers started talking to one another. To his great surprise, Errol
found that he could understand what they were saying. They spoke
a language quite similar to a language spoken on another nearby
island, a language he already knew.

And then, to his horror, Errol began to understand what the
three strangers were planning. This is what they said:

"He looks nice and big, enough for everyone, don't you think?"

"Yes. Such firm muscle. He should taste very good."

"But I would like the brains. I always get the brains. They're the
best part."

"Okay. You can have the brains. Let's get on with it, then."

The three strangers were *cannibals*: people who eat other people.
They started to walk toward Errol. Only now did Errol see that they
carried clubs, knives, and ropes in their hands.

Errol tried to run, but they were too quick for him. When he
came to, he found himself quite naked and trussed up like a turkey.
They had suspended him from a long pole. Under the pole were
logs and kindling ready for a fire.

It looked like they were planning to barbecue him.

Errol turned his head to get a better look around him. He now saw that he was in a large room. Surrounding him were many more of the strangely dressed people. They stared back at him in silence. Some were licking their lips.

Then a woman stepped forward. She was carrying a big knife.

"Wait!" said Errol.

Everyone gasped. The cannibals were surprised that Errol could speak their language.

"Please don't eat me," said Errol.

"Why should we not eat you?" asked the woman with the knife.

"Because it's wrong. Don't you see?" said Errol.

"No. I don't see. Why is it wrong?"

"You don't need to eat me, do you? You all look very well fed to me. Eat something else. Some roots, or grain, or a bird, or something."

The woman looked puzzled. "But we like eating people. They taste good! Why shouldn't we eat them?"

"Well, why don't you eat each other then?"

"But none of us wants to die. So it is better that we eat you instead."

"But I don't want to die! I am a living thing! I am enjoying my life! Don't you see? It is very wrong to end my life just so you can enjoy eating me."

Some of the others were nodding.

"Perhaps he is right," said one of them.

Errol thought he was beginning
to convince them not to eat him.
But then the woman with the knife
bent down. She put her hand into
Errol's knapsack and pulled out a
bottle of lemonade and a brown
paper bag. Out of the paper bag
fell a half-eaten sandwich.

"What is this, then?"

"Er. That's my lunch."

"What is it?"

"It's a sandwich. A beef sandwich."

"This beef was part of a living animal?"

"Yes. I suppose it was."

"It was a living thing. It enjoyed life. It didn't want to die. Yet it
was killed so you could enjoy eating its flesh."

Errol could see what she was getting at.

"Yes, But that's just an animal. It's all right to eat animals. But not
humans. Humans are different."

"But humans are animals, too. Why is it wrong to eat human
animals, if it's not wrong to eat nonhuman animals?"

Errol wasn't sure what to say to the cannibal woman's question.

"It just is. Don't you see?"

But they couldn't see. "No. We don't understand. Please explain."

What Errol needed to come up with was some reason why it
was okay to kill and eat a cow, but not okay to kill and eat a human
animal.

You know what? Errol couldn't think of a good reason. So
they killed him and cooked him. Then they ate him. After they
had eaten Errol, the cannibals went through his things. They
found some rather nice chocolate-covered mints. So they sat
around eating the mints and chatting.

The big question

The question the cannibals asked Errol was: *Why is it wrong to kill and eat human animals, but not wrong to kill and eat nonhuman animals?*

Of course, many people agree with Errol that, while it is very wrong to kill and eat a human, there is nothing wrong with killing and eating other sorts of animals.

But there are also many people who believe that, if it is wrong to kill and eat humans, then it must be wrong to kill and eat non-humans, too. They would say that it is *always* wrong to kill an animal just so we can enjoy eating it, no matter what sort of animal it is.

Now I eat meat. But should I? Am I doing something morally wrong? If I believe that it is wrong to kill and eat humans (and I *do* believe that is wrong), but not wrong to kill and eat nonhumans, it seems I must come up with some difference between humans and nonhumans that justifies my treating them so differently.

But *what is that difference?* That's my big question for this chapter. It's the question Errol couldn't answer.

Vegetarians

As I say, there are many people who believe it is wrong to kill *any* sort of animal just so we can eat it. Many of these people are *vegetarians*. They eat only vegetables, fruit, beans, nuts, grain, and so on, plus certain animal products like milk, cheese, and eggs.

Some people go even further: they don't eat or use any animal products at all. They don't even wear leather shoes. These people are called *vegans*.

Other reasons for being a vegetarian

Not *all* vegetarians give up meat because they think it is morally wrong to kill an animal just so we can enjoy eating it. There are other reasons why people become vegetarians.

Here is one of them. Many people think that a chicken farm looks like this:

But in fact most of the chickens we eat are raised in conditions much like this:

This sort of farming is sometimes called *factory farming*, because it involves mass-producing animals in much the same way that a car factory mass-produces cars.

Chickens raised in this way often never see the sky. They never see a tree. They only ever see the thousands of other chickens all around them.

This seems to many vegetarians to be a pretty cruel and unpleasant way to treat other living creatures. They also claim that the mass production of other sorts of animal for food is often also pretty unpleasant.

So here is another reason many vegetarians give when asked why they don't eat meat. They say that, while it may be wrong to slaughter animals for their meat, it is doubly wrong to raise and keep them in the cruel and barbaric way that we do. We shouldn't do it.

However, in this chapter, I am just going to focus on just this reason vegetarians give for not eating meat: *it is morally wrong to kill an animal just so we can enjoy eating it*. I will call those who give up meat for at least this reason "moral" vegetarians. Let's now get a bit clearer about what "moral" vegetarians do and don't object to.

The case of Zoe the hunter

Much of the meat we eat is produced by farms and factories. But there are a few exceptions.

This is Zoe, a tough and wily hunter who lives in the woods.

Zoe never eats meat except the deer she has shot and killed herself. She hunts only wild deer. There are plenty in the woods where she lives. Zoe makes sure she always

gets a clean, painless kill. The animal doesn't suffer at all. And she always shoots mature animals that have had a fairly long and happy life.

Is Zoe wrong to do what she does?

True, the deer Zoe eats are not produced through cruelty and suffering as factory-farmed chickens are alleged to be. So there wouldn't be that particular moral reason not to kill and eat them.

But the "moral" vegetarian would say that Zoe is still doing something morally wrong. They say that it is always wrong to deliberately bring to an end the life of a conscious, living thing —a creature capable of enjoying life—just so that someone can enjoy the taste of its flesh.

The case of Harry's road accident

What about this case? Harry is a careful driver. But one night he had a road accident. He accidentally ran over and killed a wild deer in his car while driving home at night. There was nothing he could do. The deer just ran right out in front of him.

Would it be okay for Harry to eat this deer? After all, the animal was killed accidentally.

Actually, those vegetarians who are vegetarians solely because they believe it wrong to slaughter an animal just so we can enjoy eating its meat wouldn't object to Harry's eating the deer. They would say it was a shame that the deer was killed. But they wouldn't say Harry had done something morally wrong. The point is, Harry didn't *deliberately* kill the deer so that it could be eaten. Its death was an accident.

So it's worth remembering that "moral" vegetarians needn't say that it's *always* morally wrong to eat meat.

The plane-crash cannibals

There is one animal that we would all agree is wrong to kill for its meat: the human animal. Almost no one thinks it's morally acceptable to kill humans so that we can eat them (except for those cannibals that ate Errol, of course).

But actually, I think most of us would think it okay to eat human meat if the person had been killed accidentally and it was a matter of either eating human meat or starving to death. Sometimes this does happen.

A few years ago there was an airplane crash high up in the Andes.

The survivors were left stranded high up on a mountain in all the snow and ice. They were miles from anywhere. No one came to rescue them. After a while, what little food they had ran out. They began to starve. If they didn't eat, they would die.

So the plane-crash survivors ate the bodies of the other people who had died in the crash. That's how they managed to stay alive. It was a pretty *revolting* thing for them to have to do. But I don't think it was morally wrong. And of course, the "moral" vegetarian wouldn't object, either. (By the way, I have heard it said that human meat tastes a bit like chicken and that the forearm is the best bit.)

So far, we have looked at the cannibal's question: why is it wrong to kill and eat humans for their meat, but not wrong to kill and eat nonhumans? We have also looked at "moral" vegetarians who argue that it is always wrong to deliberately kill an animal capable of enjoying life just so that we can eat it.

Is the "moral" vegetarian right? I'm not sure. I have to admit: I find it very difficult to explain why it isn't morally wrong to kill and eat nonhumans if it is morally wrong to kill and eat humans.

Let's now look at some of the arguments used to defend eating meat.

A restaurant argument

Not long ago I was at a restaurant with Aisha and Carol, two friends of mine.

Carol was eating a burger.

Carol and Aisha ended up having an argument about the morality of eating meat. The argument went like this.

CAROL: Mmm. This burger is delicious!

AISHA: That's terrible! That was a conscious, living thing, Carol. And its life was ended just so you could enjoy eating its muscles and other bits mashed up and grilled in a bun. What a waste.

CAROL: But I *like* meat. Why shouldn't I eat meat if I want to?

AISHA: Because it's *wrong*, Carol. It's wrong to kill a living thing capable of enjoying life just so that you can enjoy eating it. You could have had a veggie burger instead, like me. They are just as good.

CAROL: No, they're not. They re all mushy and taste weird. I prefer the real thing.

Carol kept eating her burger. But Aisha sat watching her. She looked very disapproving. After a while, Carol got fed up with Aisha looking at her like that. Carol started trying to defend eating meat.

Carol's first argument: It must be okay because almost everyone thinks it is

Here is Carol's first argument.

CAROL: Look, Aisha. Most people agree with me, not with you. They don't think there is anything particularly wrong about eating meat. They don't feel bad about it. If there really were something morally wrong with eating meat, then people would feel bad about it, wouldn't they? So there can't be anything wrong with it.

Aisha wasn't convinced.

AISHA: I agree that most people in this country don't think it's wrong to kill animals just so we can enjoy eating their flesh. But just because they are in the majority doesn't make them right. After all, not so very long ago there were many countries where the majority thought that *slavery* was morally acceptable. They thought certain races of people were inferior and that people of these races could therefore be used as slaves by the rest of us.

Nowadays, we see that slavery is very wrong. So the majority were simply mistaken about what is wrong. The majority may be mistaken about the morality of eating meat, too.

I agree with Aisha. Just because most people think it's okay to kill and eat animals doesn't make it right. Perhaps one day—in, say, two hundred years' time—we will look back on how we treat animals and be horrified, just as we are now horrified by slavery. Perhaps we will then see that what the majority of us now find morally acceptable is actually very wrong indeed.

Carol's second argument: It is natural to eat meat

Carol didn't give up. She came up with a second argument to defend eating meat.

> CAROL: Look, Aisha, it is *natural* for us to eat meat. We are *designed* to eat meat.

Carol opened her mouth and showed Aisha the two pointed teeth that come down from the corners of her mouth.

CAROL: See these two teeth? These are *canine* teeth. You have them, too. They are *designed* for eating meat. All meat-eating creatures have them. I'm just doing what comes naturally.

But Aisha didn't think that was any reason not to be a vegetarian.

AISHA: So what? So what if it comes naturally to us to eat meat? That doesn't make it *right,* does it? Many of the things that come naturally to us are morally wrong. What about fighting and murdering one another? That sort of behavior also seems to come quite naturally to us humans. But that doesn't mean it is morally acceptable. We don't *need* to eat meat. We can get by quite well on a vegetarian diet. So we shouldn't eat meat. What you are doing is *wrong.*

Again, I think Aisha is right: just because it comes naturally to us to eat meat doesn't mean that it is morally acceptable.

Some people would also argue that not only is it natural for humans to eat meat, it is unhealthy for us not to. We need meat to keep us healthy. But it is unclear whether this is true. There are many millions of vegetarians all over the world. Jains, Buddhists, and Hindus don't eat meat. And Jains, Buddhists, and Hindus all seem pretty healthy.

In any case, even if it were true that we need to eat some meat to keep us in the peak of condition, we don't need to eat nearly as much meat as we do. And even if a bit of meat is required for perfect health, that doesn't mean that we should eat it. We could develop food supplements instead: tablets that contain what it is that we are missing out on by not eating meat. Even if such tablets could not be made, that still wouldn't mean that it was morally acceptable to eat meat. Perhaps we should just put up with being slightly less healthy than we might otherwise be. Maybe that is the price we have to pay for doing the right thing.

But, as I say, it isn't at all clear that being a vegetarian is less healthy than eating meat.

Carol's third argument: Animals are bred to be eaten

Carol sat chewing in silence for a while. She certainly didn't think that what she was doing was wrong. So she tried a third argument.

> **CAROL:** Okay, Aisha, you are concerned about conscious living things, right?
>
> **AISHA:** Yes. I don't think a living thing capable of enjoying life should be deliberately killed just because we feel like eating it.
>
> **CAROL:** But this animal that I am eating was *bred* to be eaten. It only had life because we bred it.
>
> **AISHA:** That's true, I suppose.
>
> **CAROL:** We meat-eaters gave life to the animal. So, in a way, we did the animal a favor. True, we brought its life to an early end so that we could eat it. But still, a life existed that would not have existed if we didn't eat meat. So, on balance, breeding animals for slaughter is a *good* thing, not a bad thing.
>
> **AISHA:** No. You are wrong. Look, suppose that there are some Martian creatures who are farmers. These farmers breed humans. The Martians are quite considerate farmers. They breed humans on a planet—planet Earth—where the human animals can lead happy, fulfilled lives. Just like the cows in a field, we humans don't realize we're being bred.
>
> **CAROL:** Why are the Martians breeding us humans?
>
> **AISHA:** Because they like to eat us! You know when humans sometimes just disappear? Actually, they are abducted by Martians. They are eaten. The Martians come over here in their flying saucers to stock up on meat in just the same way that we drive over to the supermarket.

There is nothing a Martian likes better than to tuck into a nice, juicy human burger at the end of a long day.

SPECIAL
CHEESE HUMAN BURGER
IN A BUN WITH FRIES

CAROL: Yuck. That is horrible! Honestly, I'm eating. Couldn't you at least wait until I finish?

AISHA: So you find that horrible, do you?

CAROL: Yes, I do.

AISHA: Well, take a look at yourself. There you are eating an animal that has been bred and killed just so you could enjoy the taste of it in a bun. Why is that any less horrible? I think it is just as horrible.

CAROL: No, it isn't.

AISHA: You said that it was okay to eat animals because they are bred to be eaten. Well, in my story the Martians breed us to be eaten, too. So what's wrong with the Martians eating us?

Carol's fourth argument: Animals are stupid

CAROL: Okay. I admit the fact that animals are bred to be eaten doesn't by itself make it right to eat them. But animals are different from us. They are less intelligent than us. They don't have feelings like we do. They have no sense of right or wrong. That's why it's okay for us to kill and eat them.

What do you think about this argument? Does the fact that animals aren't as smart as us, aren't as emotionally sophisticated as us, don't have any sense of right or wrong, and so on, mean that it is okay for us to eat them? Aisha certainly didn't agree.

AISHA: So it's all right to eat things that are less intelligent than us? It's all right to eat things that don't have all the same sorts of feelings as us?

CAROL: Yes.

AISHA: Well, suppose that, perhaps because of some sort of illness, many human babies are born different from the rest of us. They aren't as intelligent. They are only as intelligent as a fairly intelligent animal: a pig, say. They cannot learn language. Like pigs, they can feel happy or sad, excited or calm, and so on. But they can't feel a sophisticated emotion like pride in a new job. They don't even know what a job is. Nor have they any sense of right or wrong.

CAROL: The poor things.

AISHA: Well, don't feel too bad for them. These babies are perfectly healthy, happy individuals. They are capable of living long and happy lives. So how should we treat these human beings, do you think?

CAROL: We would probably give them lots of care and attention. We would probably employ people to help them lead the most fulfilled and enjoyable lives possible.

AISHA: But why not *kill and eat them*? After all, you said that it was okay to eat animals because they are less intelligent and sophisticated than us. But so are these humans. So why shouldn't we kill and eat them, too?

Carol was absolutely revolted by the thought of eating these humans. But she was more than just revolted. She saw that it would be morally very wrong to kill and eat them.

The problem was that Carol was beginning to find it difficult to explain why it would be morally wrong to kill and eat these humans if it wasn't morally wrong to kill and eat the animals we eat. These humans were no more intelligent or sophisticated than were those animals.

CAROL: Look, Aisha. It's just a fact that humans are more important than animals. Our needs and desires come first. That is just the way it is. Human beings are more important than animals.

AISHA: But why are they more important, Carol? You haven't given me any good reason why they don't deserve the very same sort of moral consideration as we human animals do. And if you can't explain why they aren't deserving of equal consideration, then your claim is just a prejudice. It seems to me that you are prejudiced against nonhuman animals in the same way that some people are prejudiced against women or against other races of humans.

Carol winced. She didn't like to think of herself as being prejudiced.

AISHA: And in any case, even if it *is* true that human animals *are* more important, that doesn't justify our killing and eating other sorts of animal. It doesn't mean we have the right to do just what we like to them. It doesn't mean it is morally okay for us to slaughter them just because we like the taste of their flesh.

Carol now felt quite guilty. So did I. I had just eaten a burger, too. My conscience was starting to bother me. Like Carol, I hadn't really thought about the morality of eating meat before. I felt that Aisha was probably wrong about its being immoral to eat meat. But I couldn't see why she was wrong.

Pets

I had also started thinking about pets. Carol has a dog. It is a very cute dog: Tigger. Now a dog is an animal like any other. Yet Carol would be absolutely horrified at the thought that we might kill

Tigger and eat him. In fact, Carol has had to spend a lot of money on Tigger keeping him alive. Tigger swallowed a plastic pen top, which got stuck inside him. The vet had to operate to remove the pen top. The operation cost a fortune. Carol was very upset when she thought Tigger might die. Aisha and I had to comfort her while the operation was taking place. Luckily, Tigger survived. He's fine now.

Now a dog is a very intelligent and emotional creature. But apparently it is no more intelligent or emotional than a pig. That's what friends who have kept pigs tell me, anyway. Apparently, pigs are very bright, affectionate creatures. Some varieties of pig can even make quite good pets.

In some countries—China, for example—dogs are eaten. They eat dogs just as we eat pigs. And why not? There really is no difference, except perhaps that dogs look a bit more cuddly to us.

I couldn't help thinking how Carol would react if she were told that it was Tigger that she had just eaten. Carol would certainly feel it would be morally wrong to kill and eat Tigger. But then why wasn't it morally wrong to kill and eat that cow that she had just eaten?

I thought it was probably best not to ask Carol why we shouldn't eat Tigger.

Carol's fifth argument: Animals eat animals

Carol, Aisha, and I all ordered ice cream. While we were eating it, Carol had another attempt at defending herself.

CAROL: Animals eat each other, don't they? Cats eat mice and birds. Tigers eat gazelles. Foxes eat chickens. So if animals eat one another, why shouldn't we eat them, too?

AISHA: Animals don't know any better. They don't know right from wrong. They have no sense of morality. So they can't be held morally responsible for what they do, any more than newborn babies. But we adult humans can be held morally responsible. Eating meat is wrong. Once we see that, we should stop doing it. If we don't stop doing it, that makes us bad people.

I have to say I now felt very guilty about having eaten meat. So did Carol. But should we have felt guilty? Was Aisha justified in attacking us as she did? I'm not sure. I have to admit, her arguments did seem very powerful.

How could Carol and I have defended ourselves against Aisha? Why is it okay to kill and eat nonhuman animals, but not human animals?

It is the species that matters

Some people claim that it is the species one belongs to that is important, so far as what is morally acceptable to kill and eat is concerned. It is morally wrong to eat members of the human species. It is not morally wrong to eat the members of other animal species.

But *why* is it wrong to eat the members of the human species, but not other species? Isn't this just a prejudice of ours? Or can this claim be justified? Some try to explain why it is wrong to eat members of the human species but not other species by saying that humans *as a species* are more intelligent and emotionally sophisticated than other animal species. Even if some particular human being happens not to be as intelligent or emotionally sophisticated as the rest of us (like one of the babies in Aisha's example), it is still wrong to eat that particular human. It is wrong because they are members of the human species, and humans *as a species* are far more intelligent and emotionally sophisticated than other animal species. The pig, on the other hand, is a relatively stupid and unsophisticated species. So it is okay to eat pigs.

I have worries about this view, too. One of my worries is illustrated by the case of the smart pig.

The case of the smart pig

Suppose there was a talking pig, like the pig in the film. I know that there aren't really talking pigs. But just suppose that, by some miracle, such a pig was born.

This pig is one of a kind. It is incredibly intelligent: more intelligent than most humans. It is also capable of all the emotions that we are capable of. It engages us in philosophical debate about moral issues. It writes poetry. It tells insightful jokes. It enjoys reading Shakespeare and going to the theater.

It gets invited to dinner parties.

Would it be morally acceptable to kill and eat this pig? We have not yet been given any reason why it would be wrong to eat it, since it is a member of a species that normally is pretty stupid and unsophisticated compared to human beings. It is a member of the pig species.

Yet surely it would be wrong to eat this particular pig. In fact, it seems to me that this pig would be a person, despite not being a human person. And it would surely be wrong to kill and eat a person.

So my worry is this. If it is morally okay to eat animals which are members of species that are fairly unintelligent, then it should be morally acceptable to kill and eat this pig. But clearly it would not be morally acceptable to kill and eat this pig.

Are we bigots?

Some philosophers argue that many of us are guilty of *species discrimination* or *speciesism*. Species discrimination is a bit like sexual discrimination (sexism) or racial discrimination (racism). It is an example of bigotry: unreasoned prejudice against those who are different.

We discriminate against other animal species in many ways: one way is that we think that it's morally acceptable to kill and eat those other species, but not to kill and eat our own species.

But there is no justification for our discriminating against other species of animal in this way. The discrimination is unfair and immoral. Speciesism is no more morally acceptable than sexism or racism. Just as we now see that sexism and racism are wrong, so we will hopefully one day come to see that speciesism is wrong, too.

That is how some philosophers argue, at least. Are these philosophers right? What do you think?

The "it's no big deal" excuse

Some people argue that "moral" vegetarians are making a big fuss about very little. Take a look at the world. People are tortured and killed every day. Children are forced to work long hours in appalling conditions for just a few pennies. Some even starve. There are so many terrible moral injustices that cry out for our attention. Even if we admit that killing other animals so that we can enjoy eating their flesh is morally wrong, it's just one wrong among countless others. So isn't it rather narrow-minded of "moral" vegetarians to focus on just this one issue?

I think this is a very poor argument against "moral" vegetarianism. Of course, many "moral" vegetarians are concerned about all these other issues, too. Just because one is concerned about one thing doesn't mean one can't be concerned about anything else.

Really, people who argue in this way are just trying to excuse themselves. They are saying, "Okay, I admit I am doing something morally wrong. But look at all the other terrible things people do! Set against all these other terrible moral wrongs, my eating meat is rather insignificant, isn't it?"

Of course, if this were an acceptable defense, then in much the same way you could excuse all sorts of terrible things, from stealing a book to murdering someone. How would you feel about people who tried to excuse themselves for having murdered someone they didn't like by saying, "It was just one little murder! That's not so bad!"

Perhaps a better way for meat eaters to try to excuse themselves is to say that, compared to other immoral acts, killing animals for food is pretty low down on the scale of badness. Some things are more wrong than others. At the top of the scale is killing thousands or millions of people, like Hitler or Pol Pot. Further down the scale is deliberately killing a person. Further down still is killing someone accidentally through stupidity (such as running them over while drunk). Further down from that is stealing someone's life savings. Then there is stealing some sweets from a shop. Near the bottom of the scale is, say, picking an apple from a neighbor's tree without asking him first. Now on this scale of wrongs, eating meat is pretty low down, right? Even if we admit that killing other animals so we can enjoy eating them is morally wrong, surely it isn't *that* wrong.

In fact, isn't there something rather offensive about "moral" vegetarians who make such a big deal about animal exploitation and suffering? Isn't human exploitation and suffering far more important?

Are we as bad as the slave owners?

How good an excuse is the "It's no big deal" excuse? Most vegetarians would say: not very. Here's why.

Perhaps, in two hundred years' time, people will look back at our treatment of animals today and be quite horrified. Perhaps they will say to themselves: how did we not see that breeding billions and billions of animals per year in barbaric conditions and then slaughtering them just so that we could enjoy the taste of their flesh was an *absolutely monstrous* thing to do? How did we not see that what we were doing was not terribly morally wrong?

Looking back at slavery, we find it very hard to see how people back then didn't realize that how they were treating other human beings was very wrong. In fact, some treated their slaves no better than their animals, sometimes worse. They whipped them, tortured them, and kept them in appalling conditions. Some slave owners deliberately crippled their slaves when they tried to run away. How could those slave owners not see that their behavior toward these other human beings was wrong? Yet the slave owners didn't see it. Most of the slave owners thought of themselves as upright, moral citizens.

So maybe we are like the slave owners. Perhaps we are simply blind to the wrongness of what we are doing. Because we are surrounded by many other people who also think it okay to treat animals as we do, we find it difficult to see that what we are doing is wrong.

I have tried to explain why I am suspicious about the claim that, while eating meat is morally wrong, it isn't *that* wrong. Perhaps it really is very wrong indeed. Perhaps the only reason it doesn't *seem* that wrong is that the majority of other people around us feel quite comfortable with the idea.

And in fact we haven't yet seen any reason to suppose killing other species of animal for their meat isn't very wrong. Indeed, we haven't yet seen any reason to suppose it isn't just as bad as killing human animals for their meat.

Carol's final argument: Shouldn't Aisha be a vegan?

Let's go back to Carol and Aisha's argument. I felt that Aisha had definitely been getting the better of the argument up to now. But then Carol came up with a much better argument that stopped Aisha in her tracks. This is what Carol said:

CAROL: That was great ice cream.

AISHA: Mmm. I love ice cream.

CAROL: So Aisha, tell me: *why isn't it morally wrong to eat ice cream?* After all, ice cream is made from milk, which comes from cows. And cheese comes from cows, too. You had cheese on your veggie burger.

AISHA: But cows aren't *killed* to make cheese and ice cream.

CAROL: But aren't they sometimes kept in quite miserable conditions?

AISHA: I don't know. Perhaps they are.

CAROL: Look. Even if they are well looked after, don't they still have to have calves before they can make milk?

AISHA: Yes. I suppose that's right.

CAROL: So what happens to all those calves then? Half of them are male, so they are no good for milking.

AISHA: Er. Yes.

CAROL: They are *killed,* aren't they? They would have to be. Otherwise we would be up to our necks in bulls.

AISHA: Umm. I suppose you are right.

CAROL: Well, then. Here you are lecturing me about eating my burger. But it's only because I had a burger that you could have that ice cream and that cheese on your veggie burger. You are a hypocrite! Also, I bet you are wearing leather shoes, aren't you?

AISHA: Yes.

CAROL: And where did the leather for your shoes come from? Another dead animal. So you see, you are just as responsible for the deaths of all these animals as I am, despite the fact that you don't eat meat!

It is true that, in order to continue to produce milk, cows need to become pregnant once a year. Only about a quarter of their calves go on to provide milk. The rest are killed. And even those cows that are used for milk are slaughtered at three to seven years (cows can live for much longer than this). So milk production certainly does require that a great many animals be killed.

I was quite impressed by Carol's argument: if Aisha really was convinced about the immorality of killing animals, then it seems she should also give up milk and cheese and ice cream. She should give up leather, too. She should wear plastic or cotton shoes.

As I explained at the beginning of this chapter, some people called *vegans*—do go this far. They give up all animal produce. If Aisha were convinced by her own arguments, it seems she should become a vegan. Yet Aisha never did become a vegan. To this day, she still wears leather shoes. She still eats cheese, milk, eggs, and ice cream.

Still, all Carol has shown, at best, is that Aisha is a bit of a hypocrite. All she has shown is that, if it is wrong to kill and eat animals for their meat, then it's also wrong to kill them for their milk, eggs, leather, and so on. Notice that Carol hasn't shown that it is morally acceptable to kill and eat other species of animal. She still hasn't given us any reason to suppose that killing animals for meat, milk, eggs, and leather isn't *very wrong indeed*.

Should I eat meat?

I have tried to look at the arguments for and against vegetarianism and veganism as fairly as I can. I have not tried to push you one way or the other. I want you to think carefully about the arguments and make up your own mind.

I eat meat. But I have to admit, I find the moral arguments for not eating meat to be very powerful. If it is morally okay to kill and eat other species of animal just because we like the taste of their flesh, then why is it okay? If we cannot justify treating other species so very differently from our own, then it seems we really are guilty of speciesism.

Question 5

Can I jump in the same river twice?

Aisha's amazing philosophical "discovery"

Not long ago Aisha and Carol went down to the river near where they live. They went for a swim. Then they sat at a picnic table and ate their sandwiches.

Aisha was looking at the river and thinking to herself. Suddenly, she became very excited.

AISHA: I've just made an amazing philosophical discovery!
CAROL: What is it?
AISHA: You can't jump in the same river twice!
CAROL: Don't be silly! Of course you can.
AISHA: I'm not being silly. Look, suppose you jump into that river over there. . . .

Splosh. Then you get out. And then you jump back in a second time. The river will have changed in many ways between your jumping in the first time and your jumping in the second, right?

Carol wasn't sure about this.

CAROL: Hmm. Why?
AISHA: Well, it's obvious. Water will have flowed down the river. So the river won't contain exactly the same water. And things will have moved about in the river. The reeds will have moved.

The fish will
have swum
around. . . .

The mud on the bottom will have been churned about a bit. . . .

That sort of thing. The river will have changed.

Carol agreed that the river would have changed in these different ways.

AISHA: Well then, if the river has changed, then it is *not the same,* is it?
CAROL: I suppose not.
AISHA: And if it's not the *same* river, then there are *two* rivers, not one. There is the river you jump into the first time. And then

there is a second, different, river that you jump into the second time. Don't you agree?

Common sense

Carol wasn't sure she did agree.

> **CAROL:** Uh . . . no. That's not right. *Of course*, you can jump into the same river twice. I mean, that's just common sense.
>
> **AISHA:** *Common sense?* Phooey! What does common sense know? Common sense has been shown to be wrong about many things. A few hundred years ago it was the common-sense view that the sun goes around the earth. That's what everyone believed. If you had said that the earth goes around the sun, people would have thought you were mad. But the sun *doesn't* go around the earth, does it? The earth goes around the sun.
>
> **CAROL:** Yes. Of course.
>
> **AISHA:** Well, then. Common sense *can* be wrong, can't it? And common sense is also wrong about its being possible to jump in the same river twice. In fact, I've just *proved* that common sense is wrong. I think I may be a genius!

Jumping back in very quickly

Carol sat silently. She helped herself to another sandwich. Then she had a thought.

> **CAROL:** Wait a minute. What if I were to jump in, get out, and then jump in again *really, really quickly? Then* it would still be the same river, wouldn't it?
>
> **AISHA:** No, I'm afraid not.
>
> **CAROL:** Why not?

AISHA: Because the river will still have changed, even if only a tiny bit. It's changing all the time. Even after just a tiny bit of a second it has changed. So it won't be the same when you jump in the second time, even if you do jump in very, very soon after jumping in the first time.

Carol took a bite of sandwich and made a face. She was now getting very frustrated. In fact, Carol was now so frustrated that she started to speak with her mouth full, spraying crumbs everywhere.

CAROL: Yeth. But there jutht *aren't* two wiverth, are there? I mean, the wiver you jump into first doethn't *dithappear*, does it?

AISHA: Yes, it does disappear! It's amazing, isn't it? The second there's a change, the river is gone! It no longer exists! It is replaced by a *new* river. And the second there's another change, no matter how tiny, that river is gone, too, to be replaced by a third river. And so on. You see, in each case, once there is a change, no matter how small, the river is different. It's not the same. And if it's not the same river, then it must be a new river that takes the old river's place.

Aisha pointed over at the river flowing gently past them.

AISHA: Look at that river. What you are actually looking at are many rivers—*millions and millions* of rivers, in fact—each one existing only for a moment, each immediately being replaced by another river slightly different from it.

CAROL: Oh, honestly! That's just crazy. You're *nuts*!

AISHA: I'm not nuts! I've made an amazing philosophical discovery! Okay, I admit it's not common sense. But common sense can be wrong. In fact, that's *why* my discovery is amazing: it *shows* that common sense is wrong.

"I can see that the river doesn't disappear"

Carol still wasn't convinced.

CAROL: This is utterly ridiculous! Look! You can see that the river doesn't disappear! What I see with my own two eyes shows me you're wrong.

Aisha admitted that the river doesn't *seem* to disappear. But she thought the fact that the river didn't *seem* to disappear didn't prove anything:

AISHA: Look, Carol, think about your TV set.

When you look at the moving picture on the screen, what you are actually looking at is lots of still images which appear one after the other. But because each image is so similar to the one before and because they all come and go so quickly, it looks as if there is just one picture which moves.

105

CAROL: Yes. I know about that.

AISHA: Well, the same is true of this river. We are actually looking at many rivers, none of which change. But because each river is so similar to the one before and because the rivers come and go so quickly, it looks as if there is just one river that is changing.

Aisha wondered whether she had convinced Carol.

AISHA: So, Carol, do you *now* agree with me that the river you jump into the second time is a second, different river?

CAROL: I suppose so.

Actually, Carol didn't really agree at all. Carol just said she agreed because she couldn't see what was wrong with Aisha's argument. But she still felt there must be *something* wrong with the argument.

What do you think? Do you agree with Aisha or with Carol?

Aisha and Carol go bowling

Carol spent the night tossing and turning.

She was thinking about Aisha's argument. Finally, after a lot of thinking, Carol changed her mind. She decided that Aisha must be right after all. No matter how hard she tried, Carol just couldn't see anything wrong with Aisha's argument. In fact, Carol even came up with a similar argument of her own.

The next day, Carol and Aisha decided to go bowling. They met up at the bowling alley. Soon they had their bowling shoes on and were about to play their first game. As they played, Carol explained her new argument to Aisha.

CAROL: Aisha, I have also made an exciting philosophical discovery.
AISHA: What is it, then?
CAROL: You cannot meet one and the same *person* twice.
AISHA: Why not?

Carol picked up a ball and aimed it carefully at the pins. Then she released the ball. Aisha watched as Carol's ball rumbled along and noisily knocked over all the pins.

CAROL: Strike! Well, it's just like in the case of the river. You said that the river is not the same the second time you jump in. And if it is not the *same* river, then there are *two* rivers, not one. Right?
AISHA: Yes. That's right.
CAROL: Now, when you meet a person and then you meet them again later, they too will also have changed in various ways, won't they?
AISHA: I guess so.
CAROL: The person you meet the second time will be different in various ways. So they won't be the same. And if it is not the *same* person you meet, then there are *two* people that you meet, not one!

Aisha was quite impressed. She picked up a bowling ball.

AISHA: Actually, I think you're right! You know, I hadn't thought of that!

CAROL: Yes. In fact, the person you meet the first time must *disappear*! The second there's a change, they are gone forever. They are replaced by a new person. And the second there's another change, that person is gone, too, to be replaced by a third person. In each case, once there is a change, no matter how tiny, the person is different. They are not the same. So a new person must take the old person's place.

Aisha put her bowling ball down again. She had started to worry about what Carol was saying.

AISHA: But hang on. That means that you aren't the person I was talking to yesterday.

CAROL: Actually, *you* didn't exist yesterday, so *you* weren't talking to anyone yesterday! Neither of us existed yesterday! So that conversation yesterday was had by *two other people entirely*!

AISHA: That can't be right, can it?

CAROL: Yes. It is right! It seems we have made another amazing discovery! In fact, here's a second reason why I can't jump into one and the same river twice. Not only will it not be one and the same river that's jumped into the second time, the person who jumps into it *won't be me*. I won't exist anymore. The person who jumps in the second time is a brand-new person.

Aisha looked stunned. Carol picked up a bowling ball and started to aim it at the pins.

CAROL: Actually, I've just made an even more amazing discovery. Even the people who started this conversation just two minutes ago don't exist now. In fact, because we are changing all the time, *even the person that started this sentence is not the same person as the person now finishing it.* In fact . . .

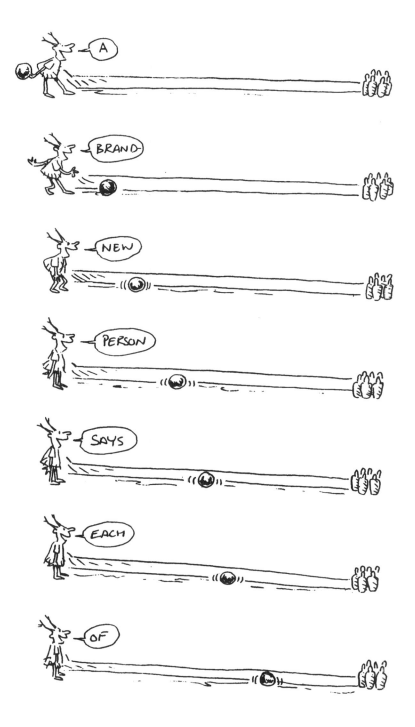

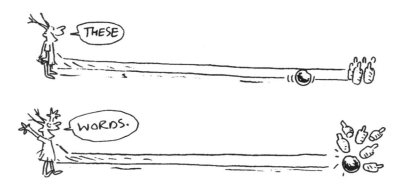

Now Aisha started to feel very unsure.

AISHA: That certainly is amazing, Carol. Actually, that seems just a bit *too* amazing. It's *downright ridiculous.* Haven't we made a mistake somewhere?

CAROL: You're not going to go back to boring old common sense now, are you? Common sense can be wrong. It's been wrong before. You said so yourself. Don't you remember?

But Aisha now felt that they must have made a mistake somewhere.

AISHA: Yes, I know I did. But now I'm not sure we should be so quick to give up common sense. To say that neither of us existed one minute ago or even just a second ago *can't* be right, surely? We *must* have gone wrong somewhere along the way.

The candy-apple incident

Aisha said she was hungry, so they walked over to the candy-apple stand and each bought a candy apple.

Aisha gulped her candy apple down right away. Carol stood holding hers while it cooled down a bit.

Suddenly, just as Carol was about to take her first bite, Aisha grabbed Carol's candy apple from out of her hands and bit a huge chunk out of it.

> CAROL: *Hey!* What do you think you're doing?
> AISHA: What's the problem?
> CAROL: You just ate *half my candy apple*! That's the problem!
> AISHA: No, I didn't.
> CAROL: Yes, you did! I just saw you!
> AISHA: Actually, you're wrong.

Carol looked like she was about to explode, so Aisha thought she had better explain.

> AISHA: Look, *I* didn't eat your candy apple. If your argument is right, *I* didn't exist two moments ago, did I?
> CAROL: Er . . . Well, no.
> AISHA: Right. So the person who ate your candy apple was another person entirely.

Aisha gave Carol back the remains of the candy apple.

> AISHA: And in any case, *you* haven't missed out on anything because the person who was about to bite into that candy apple before it was grabbed *wasn't you.* You've only existed for a tiny fraction of a second.
> CAROL: You're just being stupid!
> AISHA: I'm just pointing out that if your argument is correct, then *I* haven't done anything wrong. So why are you blaming me?

Actually, Aisha is quite right. If Carol's argument is correct, then the person who stole the candy apple isn't the person now standing in front of her. In fact, the person who stole the candy apple *no longer* exists. But that can't be right, can it? Not even Carol *really* believed that the person who stole the candy apple had ceased to exist.

Two puzzles

There are two puzzles facing Aisha and Carol. The first puzzle is this. On the one hand, it seems obvious that you *can* jump into one and the same river twice—that's the common-sense view. On the other hand, it seems Aisha has an argument that shows that you *can't* jump into one and the same river twice. The river will have changed. So it won't be the same. And if it isn't the same river, then, amazingly, it seems there must be *two* rivers, not one.

There is a similar puzzle about how you could meet the same person twice. On the one hand, the common-sense view is that you can meet the one and the same person twice; on the other hand, Carol's argument seems to show that you can't.

How are we to solve these two puzzles? Should we give up on the common-sense view? Or is there something wrong with the arguments that seem to show that common sense is wrong? But if there is something wrong with these arguments, then *what is* wrong with them? What do you think?

Heraclitus

These puzzles are very old. They may even be twenty-five hundred years old. Heraclitus, a philosopher who lived in ancient Greece, is often supposed to have claimed that one cannot jump into the same river twice.

YOU CANNOT JUMP IN THE SAME RIVER TWICE!

If that is what Heraclitus claimed, then perhaps it was an argument like Aisha's that led him to that conclusion.

I introduce myself

Let's get back to Aisha and Carol. They were now looking mad at each other. Carol ate the rest of her candy apple in silence.

Now I also happened to be at the bowling alley that day. So I decided to walk over and say hello.

> ME: I couldn't help overhearing what you two were saying. You know, about not being able to jump in the same river twice or meet the same person twice.
>
> CAROL: Sorry. We were shouting a bit, weren't we?
>
> ME: Well, anyway, I'm afraid I'm not very good at bowling.
>
> AISHA: Yes. We noticed you falling over earlier on.
>
> ME: But I think I can help you with your philosophical puzzles.
>
> CAROL: How?
>
> ME: Well, you seem to have gotten yourselves into a bit of a muddle. I think I can sort it out for you.
>
> AISHA: What muddle? What do you mean?

Two sorts of sameness

I started to explain that the words "the same" are actually used in two different ways. They are used to talk about two quite different sorts of sameness.

> ME: To get unmuddled, you need to distinguish between two sorts of sameness.

AISHA: I don't follow. What two sorts of sameness?

ME: Let me explain. Take a look at these two bowling balls.

I pointed to two bowling balls lying on the floor nearby.

ME: Those two balls are not *the same ball*, are they? There are two balls in front of us, not one. Right?

AISHA: Of course.

ME: So here is the way the balls are *not the same*: they are not *one and the same ball*. The number of balls is two, not one.

AISHA: I agree.

ME: Yet there are also many ways in which these two balls *are* the same. Both balls are round. Both are black. They weigh the same. They're both made out of the same kind of stuff. The two balls are the same in many of their qualities, aren't they?

AISHA: Yes. Of course.

ME: Now, when two things *share the same qualities* we philosophers say: they are *qualitatively* the same.

AISHA: I see.

ME: These two balls aren't qualitatively *exactly* the same in *all* their qualities, of course. There are many small differences between them, mostly too small for the eye to see. But there seems no reason why there couldn't be two balls that were exactly the same in all their qualities, right?

CAROL: No. I guess not.

ME: Now think. Suppose there are two balls that are qualitatively exactly the same in every respect. They share all the same qualities: both are black; they weigh the exact same amount. In fact, the two balls are exactly the same right down to the last atom.

These two balls are still not *one and the same ball*, are they? There are still *two* balls, not one, aren't there?

CAROL: Yes. There are two balls.

ME: Right. So here is a sense in which two balls that *are* qualitatively exactly the same are still *not* the same. They are not one and *the same* ball. We philosophers often say that they are not *numerically* the same, because the number of balls is two, not one.

AISHA: I see. You are saying there are two sorts of sameness: qualitative sameness and numerical sameness.

ME: Exactly!

CAROL: You are saying that bowling balls can be qualitatively the same without being numerically the same. Even if two balls share all the same qualities, there are still *two* balls, not one.

ME: Exactly!

Numerical sameness without qualitative sameness

In fact, not only can you have things which are qualitatively the same but not numerically the same, you can also have things that are numerically the same but not qualitatively the same, as I now explained.

> ME: Here's an example of numerical sameness without qualitative sameness. Suppose we take that black bowling ball and paint it white. Once the ball has been painted, it's not *qualitatively* the same as it was before, is it?

> CAROL: No. One of its qualities is different. It's white, not black.
> ME: Exactly. So it is not *qualitatively* the same. But it is still *numerically* the same ball. There is just *one* ball, not two, despite the fact that it has changed color.
> CAROL: Right.
> ME: Here's another example. Suppose I see a tasty cupcake on a plate in front of me.

I pull off a small bit of cupcake and eat it.

Is it now the same cupcake that's sitting on the plate in front of me?

CAROL: The cake is and isn't the same. It's *numerically* the same cake. But the cake isn't *qualitatively* exactly the same as it was before. It weighs a bit less, and it's a slightly different shape: it has a bite taken out of it.

ME: That's right! The cake is another example of something being numerically the same but not qualitatively the same. Just because I have taken a bite out of the cupcake doesn't mean the cupcake now sitting in front of me isn't *numerically* the same cupcake that was sitting there before.

AISHA: I see.

Where did Aisha go wrong?

I now explained the problem with Aisha's argument.

Aisha argued like this.

WHEN YOU JUMP IN THE SECOND TIME, THE RIVER WILL HAVE CHANGED. SO IT WON'T BE THE SAME. BUT IF IT'S NOT THE SAME RIVER, THEN THERE ARE TWO RIVERS THAT YOU JUMP INTO, NOT ONE.

Can you now see the problem with this argument? Aisha starts by pointing out, quite correctly, that the river you jump into the second time won't be *qualitatively* exactly the same as it was before. For it is, of course, true that between jumping in each time the river will have changed qualitatively in some respects: things will have moved about, the water will have flowed along, and so on. Of course, this is hardly an amazing philosophical discovery, right? It's just a pretty obvious and rather boring fact about rivers.

On the other hand, the claim that you can't jump into the same river twice *numerically* is a much more exciting claim. It is the claim that Aisha ends up making. She ends up saying that there are two rivers that you jump into, not one. It certainly would be amazing if Aisha could show that you can't jump into the *numerically* same river twice.

The problem is, of course, that Aisha has shown no such thing. Aisha's argument is a bad argument. It only looks convincing because we fail to notice that Aisha is using the words "the same" in two different ways. Yes, the river won't be *qualitatively* exactly the same as it was before. But just because the river is not *qualitatively* the same as it was before does not mean it's not *numerically* one and the same river.

Of course, Carol's argument that you cannot meet one and the same person twice is also a bad argument for exactly the same reason.

The solutions to the puzzles

So between us we solved the two puzzles.

The first puzzle was this. On the one hand, common sense says that you *can* jump into one and the same river twice. On the other hand, Aisha has an argument that seems to show that you can't jump into one and the same river twice: there must be two rivers, not one. We either had to find something wrong with Aisha's argument or else give up the common-sense view.

We can now see that here is one philosophical puzzle that does have a solution. There is something wrong with Aisha's argument. So we can stick with the common-sense view after all—at least until someone comes up with a better argument than Aisha's.

Of course, Carol's puzzle about how one could meet one and the same person twice is also solved in much the same way.

Tripped up by words

After I had explained to Aisha and Carol where they had gone wrong, we all bought milk shakes.

Carol now felt quite relieved. The two puzzles had really been starting to annoy her. But Aisha felt slightly disappointed.

CAROL: But that means that neither of us had *really* made an amazing philosophical discovery after all, doesn't it?

ME: Yes. I'm afraid so.

AISHA: I thought I was a philosophical genius. But it turns out I was just confused!

ME: That's right. You were *tricked by language*. Sometimes, when it seems to us that we have made an amazing philosophical discovery or that we face a difficult philosophical puzzle, all that's really happened is that we have been tripped up by words.

AISHA: How were we tripped up?

ME: Well, you didn't pay enough attention to how certain words are *used*. You overlooked the fact that the expression "the same" is used in more than one way.

CAROL: I see. I heard Aisha use the words "the same" and didn't notice she was using them differently each time.

ME: That's right. Aisha started off by saying that the river isn't qualitatively "the same," but then concluded that the river isn't numerically "the same" Once you spotted that Aisha was using the words "the same" in these two different ways, you saw that her argument didn't work.

A moral

There's an interesting moral to my story about Aisha and Carol. The moral is this. Sometimes, when it seems to us that we have made an amazing philosophical discovery or that we face a difficult philosophical puzzle, all that's really happened is that we have been tricked by language.

Of course, I'm not saying that all amazing philosophical "discoveries" are really just a result of our having been tricked by language. But whenever you come across such a philosophical "discovery," it's always worth bearing in mind that you *might* have been tricked by language.

Wittgenstein's philosophy

Actually, a very famous philosopher, Ludwig Wittgenstein, argued that *all* philosophical puzzles are a result of our having been tricked by language. According to Wittgenstein, what always leads us into philosophical trouble is the fact that we overlook differences in the way that language is used. He argued that the way to remove any philosophical puzzle is to look closely at these differences in use.

Our two puzzles about jumping in the same river and meeting the same person certainly fit Wittgenstein's view about philosophy. We've now seen that both resulted from our being tricked by language. In each case we overlooked the fact that the expression "the same" was being used in two different ways. That's what caused all the trouble. Once we saw that the expression "the same" was being used in two different ways, the puzzles disappeared.

But is Wittgenstein right to say that *all* philosophical puzzles are a result of our overlooking differences in the way words and other signs are used? Is he right to say that the way to remove *any* philosophical puzzle is to look closely at the different ways in which language is being used? That is something that philosophers disagree strongly about.

What do you think?

Question 6

Where do right and wrong come from?

Horrible Harriet

Meet Harriet.

Harriet is a schoolgirl. But she's not a very nice schoolgirl. She hits other schoolchildren and steals their lunch money.

She tears up library books and breaks the other children's bikes. In fact, Harriet makes the other students' lives quite miserable.

Murderous Murphy

Of course, we all do things that are wrong. Often we feel guilty about the bad things we have done. We feel that we should try to be better people than we are. Certainly, there are many things that I have done that I feel pretty guilty about and that I wish I hadn't done. And I am sure the same is true of you, too. No one is perfect.

While many of the things that Harriet has done are wrong, there are things that are worse. Take Murphy, for example. Murphy is a cowboy. He is also a murderer. Murphy shoots and kills defenseless travelers so he can steal their money. Here's Murphy killing some poor unarmed cowboy who was on his way back home to his family.

Killing another person is, of course, considered to be one of the very worst things that a person can do.

Morality

By saying that some of the things that Harriet and Murphy have done are wrong, I am talking about the *morality* of what they did. Harriet and Murphy *should* not have done what they did.

Of course, morality is not just about what we shouldn't do. It is also about what we *should* do. It is about doing the *right* thing. Suppose Mr. Black borrows Mr. Brown's Big Bouncer.

But while Mr. Black is riding on the Big Bouncer, he gets a bit carried away and punctures it.

What should Mr. Black do? He thinks about throwing the Big Bouncer back into Mr. Brown's garden when Mr. Brown isn't looking and running off before Mr. Brown finds out. But Mr. Black does the right thing. He admits to Mr. Brown that he punctured the Big Bouncer. He agrees to fix it.

Repaying debts, helping people in trouble, telling the truth—these are other examples of doing the *right* thing.

When we talk about morality—about right and wrong—we are talking about how we *should* live our lives. Most of us feel that it is morally wrong to lie, cheat, steal, and kill. We feel we should be honest and trustworthy. We feel we should treat other people with respect.

Morality and the law

It is important not to get morality—right and wrong—confused with the law. Of course, morality and the law do often coincide. For example, stealing and killing are both morally wrong. They are also both against the law. But morality and the law do not necessarily coincide.

Take the *apartheid* laws in South Africa not so long ago. These laws separated black people from white people. They treated black people as second-class citizens. Black people weren't allowed to vote, for example. They were only allowed to live in certain poor, run-down areas. Many things in South Africa were for whites only.

But while it might have been against the law for black people to

live in certain areas or use certain things, it wasn't *morally wrong* for them to do so. In fact, in South Africa it was the *law* that was wrong. So just because something is illegal doesn't mean it is wrong.

There are also things that are morally wrong that aren't against any law. For example, suppose Toby, a handsome and greedy young man, is told by one of his friends at a party that the sick-looking woman over there is very ill and will soon die.

Toby is also told that the woman is a bit clueless, but very nice and immensely rich. And she has no living relatives. So, despite actually finding the woman rather ugly and dull, Toby spends the evening pretending to find her fascinating and beautiful. Why? Because Toby wants to trick the woman into marrying him. He wants to trick her into leaving him all her money.

Now, most people would say that Toby's behavior is morally very wrong.

But, of course, what Toby is doing isn't *illegal*. Even if Toby did manage to trick the woman into marrying him, he wouldn't have broken any law. So what's morally wrong isn't always illegal.

Is it always wrong to kill?

We all think that killing is wrong. But is killing *anything* wrong? What about a sheep, a flea, or a blade of grass? Of course, most people would say that there's nothing wrong with killing these sorts of things. They would say that it is only other people that we shouldn't kill.

But is it *always* wrong to kill another person? Think about this case. Suppose you are a rancher in the old Wild West. Murderous Murphy breaks into your house. He dusts himself off, points his two

six-shooters at you and your family, and says that he is going to kill all of you and steal all your money.

Suppose you have a gun hidden in your hand. And suppose the only way to stop Murderous Murphy from killing you all is to shoot him dead. What would you do? I'm sure you would say that you would shoot Murderous Murphy dead. In fact, I'm sure you would say that that was the *right* thing to do.

So it seems it isn't always wrong to kill another person. While we all agree that killing another person is wrong, most of us don't mean that it is always, in every case, wrong. We mean only that generally speaking, killing is wrong. There are exceptions.

It seems there are also exceptions to other moral principles. Take, for example, the moral principle that it is wrong to lie. If Murphy asked you if there was anyone else worth robbing living nearby and you knew that there was, would it be wrong to lie to him? I don't think so.

Perhaps you can think of other moral principles to which there are exceptions. For example, are there cases in which it wouldn't be wrong to steal?

Where does morality come from?

We have been talking about morality, about right and wrong. Now we come to my big philosophical question. My question is, *Where does morality come from?* People give a number of different answers to this question. We are going to look at three of them.

One answer is that *morality comes from us. We* are the source of morality, of right and wrong. Our description of some things as "right" and others as "wrong" does no more than reflect how we think or feel about them. Things aren't right or wrong independently of what we might happen to think or feel about them.

Another quite different answer is *morality comes from God.* It is God who lays down what is right and what is wrong. So even if none of us felt that what someone did is wrong, it would *still* be wrong if God says it's wrong.

A third answer to the question "Where does morality come from?" is, *things are right or wrong anyway,* no matter what we might happen to think or feel about them, or even what God might happen to think or feel about them.

What do you think?

Which of these three answers would you give? Do you think that morality reflects only how we think or feel about things? Or do you think that morality comes from God? Or do you think that things are right or wrong *anyway*, whatever we or even God might happen to think or feel about them? Let's take a closer look at these three answers to see if we can figure out which (if any) answer is correct.

Let's start with the claim that *morality comes from us*.

Answer #1: Morality comes from us

How could morality come from us? Here are two famous philosophical theories which say that morality comes from us.

Morality comes from us: The Feelings Theory

Suppose that Murderous Murphy is drinking at a bar.

Another cowboy arrives and orders a beer. Murphy notices that this other cowboy is unarmed. Murphy also notices that the other cowboy has a lot of money in his wallet.

So when the other cowboy finishes his beer and rides off into the desert, Murphy secretly follows him. Then, when Murphy is sure no one is watching, he sneaks up behind the other cowboy and shoots him in the back.

Murphy then takes the money and rides off, leaving the cowboy to die in the sand.

Now suppose I see Murphy shooting that poor unarmed cowboy in the back. I say, "What Murphy is doing is wrong!"

According to what I will call the Feelings Theory, when I say "What Murphy is doing is wrong!" I am just saying that I have certain feelings about what Murphy is doing. I am making a claim about myself. I am saying that I disapprove of what Murphy is doing.

This means that if I do disapprove, then what I say is true: Murphy is doing something wrong.

Similarly, if I see someone repaying a debt and I say, "That person is doing something right," then I am saying that I approve of what he or she is doing.

As you can see, according to the Feelings Theory, morality comes from us. We make things right or wrong by approving or disapproving of them.

Morality comes from us: the Boo-Hooray Theory

Here's another theory that also says that morality comes from us.
Philosophers often call this theory the *Boo-Hooray Theory*.

As we have just seen, according to the Feelings Theory, when I
say that something is wrong I make a claim, a claim about how I
feel. According to the Boo-Hooray Theory, on the other hand, I don't
make a claim about how I feel. I express how I feel. Let me explain
the difference.

Suppose I am about to watch a pig race.

I bet $5 on Pink Flash at 10–1. So if Pink Flash wins, I win $50.

The race begins. Pink Flash is slow to start. Then one of the
other pigs—Honking Harry—pushes Pink Flash over. I am upset
about this. I yell, "Boo to Honking Harry!"
Then Pink Flash gets up. He catches up
with the other pigs. Finally, with just
yards to go, Pink Flash noses ahead.
He wins!

I yell out, "Hooray for Pink Flash!"

Now, ask yourself, when I yell out "Hooray for Pink Flash!," is what I say *true* or *false*? Of course, it's *neither*. I am not saying something true. But neither am I saying something false. I am not making any sort of *claim*, not even a claim about how I feel.

So what *am* I doing, then, when I say, "Hooray for Pink Flash!"? I am *expressing* how I feel. I am expressing my happiness. Similarly, when I yell, "Boo to Honking Harry!," I am again expressing how I feel. I am expressing my disapproval of what Honking Harry did.

Now, according to the Boo-Hooray Theory, something similar happens when I see Murphy shoot the other cowboy and I say, "What Murphy is doing is wrong!" When I say "What Murphy is doing is wrong," it's as if I'm yelling "Boo to what Murphy is doing!" I am expressing my disapproval of what Murphy is doing.

Similarly, when I say, "Repaying one's debts is right," it's as if I am yelling, "Hooray for repaying one's debts!" I am expressing my approval of repaying one's debts. In each case I am not making a *claim* about how I feel. I'm just *expressing* how I feel.

So according to the Boo-Hooray Theory, it's *neither* true *nor* false that what Murphy is doing is wrong. According to the Boo Hooray Theory, there is *no fact of the matter* about whether what Murphy is doing is wrong (any more than there's a fact of the matter about whether what Pink Flash is doing is right).

The Vargs

We have just looked at two theories both of which say that morality comes from us: morality does no more than reflect how we *feel* about things. What do you think about these two theories? Is either theory any good?

Like most philosophers nowadays, I have worries about both theories. In order to explain one of my worries, I shall tell you about the Vargs.

This is Planet Varg, where the Vargs live.

The Vargs are intelligent beings like ourselves. And by an amazing coincidence they also speak English. They even talk about things as being "right" and "wrong."

But Vargs feel quite differently about *what* is right and wrong. Their most basic moral principle is, *Always look after number one!* All Vargs feel very strongly that each Varg should, as far as possible, try to get what it wants, even at the expense of other Vargs. So they believe it is right to steal and cheat. In fact, they even believe it is right for one Varg to kill another if this enables them to get something they want (this doesn't mean Vargs go around stealing, cheating, and killing all the time, of course: they only cheat, steal, and kill if they think they can get away with it).

Because Vargs feel that each Varg should always look after itself,

even at the expense of other Vargs, they feel that charity is wrong. In fact, if a Varg ever feels like being charitable, it soon starts feeling guilty.

Some Vargs are even religious: they believe in a god called *Vargy* from whom they maintain their morality comes. On Sunday some Vargs go to Varg church where they hear sermons on the virtues of selfishness.

Why do I mention the Vargs? Because the possibility of creatures like the Vargs raises a problem for both the Feelings Theory and the Boo-Hooray Theory.

A problem with the Feelings Theory
Why is the possibility of creatures like the Vargs a problem for the Feelings Theory? The Feelings Theory says that when I say, "What Murphy is doing is wrong," I make a claim. I claim that I disapprove of what Murphy is doing. As I do disapprove, what I say is true: Murphy is doing something wrong.

But, of course, a Varg would say "What Murphy is doing is right!" According to the Feelings Theory, when a Varg says this, it claims that it approves of what Murphy is doing. So, as it does approve, what the Varg says is true, too. We are both right! So we can happily agree with each other!

But this can't be correct, can it? When I say, "What Murphy is doing is wrong," and the Varg says, "What Murphy is doing is right," we are *contradicting* each other. Obviously, we can't *both* be right. As we are contradicting each other, the Feelings Theory must be false.

A problem with the Boo–Hooray Theory

Why are the Vargs a problem for the Boo-Hooray Theory?

According to the Boo-Hooray Theory, when I say, "What Murphy is doing is wrong," I don't make a claim. I merely *express* how I feel. It's as if I yell, "Boo to what Murphy is doing!" Similarly, when a Varg says, "What Murphy is doing is right!," it doesn't make a claim either. It merely expresses how it feels.

Now, according to the Boo-Hooray Theory, which of us—the Varg or me—is right about what Murphy is doing? Neither! There is no fact of the matter as to which of us is correct! According to the Boo-Hooray Theory, what I say is no more "true" than what the Varg says.

But isn't there a problem here for the Boo-Hooray Theory? For surely, when I say, "What Murphy is doing is wrong," I *don't* merely express how I feel. I *do* make a claim. In fact, I suppose that what I say is *true* and what the Varg says is *false*. I suppose there is a fact of the matter about whether or not killing is wrong. I suppose that the Varg is *mistaken* about this fact of the matter.

But if this is right—if when I say, "What Murphy is doing is wrong," I do make a claim, a claim that is true—then the Boo Hooray Theory must be wrong, too.

In fact, when you start to think about it, isn't it clear that morality can't come from us? It's a fact that killing is wrong *anyway*, whatever we or the Vargs might happen to feel about killing. Even if we happened to agree with the Vargs that there is nothing wrong with killing, killing would still be wrong, wouldn't it? But how can this be?

Answer #2: Morality comes from God

We are looking at the question, Where does morality come from? So far we have looked at the answer: *morality comes from us*. But it seems that this answer cannot be right. So let's now turn to a different answer.

According to many people, the reason killing is wrong *anyway*, whatever we might have to say about it, is that *God* says it's wrong. Killing is wrong because God disapproves of it. Morality comes from God.

How do we find out about right and wrong?

So how do we find out what God disapproves of? Many would say: by looking to religion and religious books such as the Bible or the Koran. For example, the Old Testament of the Bible contains the Ten Commandments, a list ten dos and don'ts which God is supposed to have carved on two stone tablets for Moses.

One of these Ten Commandments is, of course: *Thou shalt not kill.*

The Morality-Comes-from-God Argument

So does morality come from God? Are things right or wrong simply because God says so?

I heard a man talking on the radio the other day. This man laid down a challenge to people who don't believe in God. Surely, he argued, if there is no God, then there can be no real morality. If you believe in morality, then you *have* to believe in God, too. Here's the man's argument:

> IF THERE IS NO GOD TO DECIDE WHAT IS RIGHT OR WRONG, THEN WHAT IS RIGHT AND WRONG MUST BE DECIDED BY US. BUT REAL MORALITY ISN'T SOMETHING THAT WE CAN DECIDE. THERE'S AN INDEPENDENT FACT OF THE MATTER ABOUT WHAT'S RIGHT AND WRONG. SURELY IT'S WRONG TO KILL ANYWAY, NO MATTER WHAT WE HAPPEN TO SAY OR FEEL ABOUT IT. AND IF KILLING IS WRONG ANYWAY, THEN THAT CAN ONLY BE BECAUSE THERE'S A GOD WHO SAYS THAT KILLING IS WRONG. MORALITY MUST COME FROM GOD. SO IF YOU BELIEVE IN MORALITY, YOU HAVE TO BELIEVE IN GOD TOO.

Let's call this the *Morality-Must-Come-from-God Argument*. The Morality Must-Come-from-God Argument is certainly a very popular argument. I have heard much the same argument from many different people. But is the argument any good?

Suppose God had said killing is right. . . .

In fact, the Morality-Must-Come-from-God Argument isn't any good, as we shall now see.

The man on the radio claimed that killing is wrong because God says it is wrong. God actually *makes* killing wrong by saying that it is wrong.

But this means that if *God had instead said that killing is right, then it would be.* But this can't be right, can it? Ask yourself, Suppose God had said killing is right, would it have been right?

Surely not. Surely, even if God had said that we *should* kill, it would still be wrong to go round murdering people. Not even God can make killing other people right.

The man on the radio argued like this: morality can't come from us, because we can't make killing right just by saying so. What the man on the radio failed to notice is that exactly the same is true of God. Killing is also wrong no matter what God might have to say about it. So, by the same argument, morality can't come from God, either.

Answer #3: Things are right or wrong anyway

We are looking at the question, Where does morality come from?
We have now looked at two different answers to this question. The
first answer was, Morality comes from us. The second answer was,
Morality comes from God. Neither of these answers seems to be
correct. So let's now turn to the third of the three answers we are
going to look at. The third answer is, "*Things are right or wrong anyway,*"
whatever we or even God might happen to say about them.

Objective moral facts

Those who say that killing is wrong anyway, whatever we or even
God might have to say about it, are saying that it is an *objective fact*
that killing is wrong.

What is an objective fact? Here's an
example. Suppose I believed that there
is pen on the table behind me.

My belief may be true or it may be
false. Suppose my belief is true. What
makes it true is a certain corresponding
fact: the fact that there *is* a pen back
there on the table.

MY BELIEF IS TRUE

MY BELIEF IS FALSE

And this fact seems to be an *objective* fact. What I mean is that it's a fact that there's a pen on the table, whether or not I or anyone else knows there's a pen on the table, and no matter what I or anyone else might feel about it. That there's a pen on the table is a fact "out there" in the world, a fact that is there anyway, whatever anyone might think or feel about it.

Now you might suppose that it's also an objective fact that what Murderous Murphy did is wrong.

I believe that what Murphy did is wrong. And you might suppose that my belief is made true by a corresponding fact: the fact that what Murphy did is wrong. You might also suppose that this fact is an *objective* fact: it's out there *anyway*, no matter what I or anyone else (including even God) might think or feel about it. So, even if no one thought that what Murphy did was wrong, it would still be wrong.

If there are objective moral facts, then the right answer to the question, "Where does morality come from?" is, *not from us, or from God, or from anyone else for that matter*. Morality is "out there": it's independent of *all* of us.

And this does seem correct, doesn't it? Even if we and the Vargs and God had all decided that there is nothing wrong with killing . . .

. . . as a matter of fact, killing *would* still be wrong, wouldn't it? So it seems that there really are objective moral facts.

How do we detect wrongness?

Still, there are problems with the theory that there are objective moral facts. One very famous problem is: how do we *discover* these facts? Or, to put it another way, how do we *detect* this property of wrongness that acts of killing or stealing are supposed to have?

In order to explain this problem, I shall tell you a story. The story is about two Martian visitors to Earth.

The Martian visitors

One day, two Martians—Flib and Flob— arrive in my back yard.

Flib and Flob are quite similar to us. They also have eyes and ears, a mouth and nose, two arms and two legs.

Flib and Flob offer to give me a trip around town in their flying saucer. So we get in and take off. As we fly around, we look out the window at the town below us.

Flib and Flob make the flying saucer invisible so no one can see us as we skim over the rooftops. We circle around the town and look at the pigeons. Then, as we pass over a narrow street on the outskirts of town, I notice something. I see a young man trying to snatch the purse of a woman who is walking home from the store. I quickly point this out to the Martians.

"Look!" I say. "That man is trying to steal that woman's purse. That's wrong!"

But Flib and Flob just look puzzled. Flob says: "Ah, yes. Wrong. We do not understand your Earthling talk of right and wrong. Please show us the wrongness."

Where is the wrongness?

"Look!" I say, pointing down at the robber. "Can't you see that this man is doing something wrong?"

But Flib and Flob *can't* see the wrongness of what he is doing.

"No," replies Flob. "Our eyes are just like your eyes. But we find your talk of *seeing wrongness* very strange. We just can't see this thing you Earth people call wrongness. Where is the wrongness, please?"

The Martians stare at me, waiting for a reply. I'm not quite sure what they are getting at. So Flob continues.

"We have five senses just like you Earthlings. We too can see and hear. We too can smell and taste things. And we have a sense of touch just like yours. But our five senses do not allow us to detect this thing you call *wrongness*. And we find this very mysterious. What we want to know is, Where is the wrongness? Please point it out to us. Please explain to us how you humans manage to detect it. By which of your senses do you perceive it?"

Now I begin to see what Flib and Flob are getting at. Certainly, wrongness doesn't seem to be observable in the way that, say, redness is. Redness is something that you can see (you can see the redness of an apple, for example). Wrongness, on the other hand, seems to be invisible.

The DIRS scanner

I look down at the man struggling to pull the woman's purse from her hands. I have to admit, I'm not sure *how* I detect the wrongness of what he is doing. Still, I feel quite sure that the man is doing something wrong. So I have another go at explaining to the Martians the wrongness of what the robber is doing.

"Look! That man is stealing that woman's purse! You can see that, can't you?"

Flob says that they can certainly see that.

"Well, then, stealing is wrong, isn't it?"

Flib and Flob don't understand. Flib asks, "But where is the wrongness? This further thing you call wrongness is not detected by us when we observe people stealing. Nor does the wrongness show up on any of our scanning equipment."

Flib points to a huge, gunlike object in the corner of their room.

"This is the DIRS—the Detect-all Infinite Resolution Scanner. It is the most powerful and all-encompassing scanner in the whole universe. There is nothing in the natural world that the DIRS can't detect! But not even the DIRS can detect this thing you call wrongness. We will show you."

Flib and Flob aim the DIRS toward the robbery taking place on the street.

They press a red button. There is a slight humming noise as the DIRS begins to scan what is going on down below.

"See?" says Flib, pointing at the many dials on the side of the DIRS. "We just aren't picking up any wrongness. Not a sausage!"

"Please show us the wrongness," continues Flib. "We are scientists. We want knowledge. We want a complete theory of the universe. We do not want to miss anything. But this thing you call wrongness continues to evade us."

But the woman is upset. . . .

I decide to have another go at explaining about wrongness: "Look. That woman down there is very upset. That purse contains all her money. If she loses her purse, then she won't be able to buy things that she needs from the shop. Can't you see how sad and afraid she is?"

"Oh, we know all about *that*," says Flib. "We already know all about *those* facts: the fact that the man is stealing the woman's money; the fact that that is all the money she has; the fact that the man is making her unhappy and frightened. But you seem to be able to detect an *extra* fact: the fact that what the man is doing is *wrong*. If this extra fact is out there, please point it out to us. We can find no trace of it."

"Is" facts and "should" facts

I scratch my head. "What do you mean by saying that the fact that what the man is doing is wrong is an *extra* fact?"

Flob explains as follows. "Look, by saying that someone is doing something *wrong*, you Earthlings mean that they *should not* do it, don't you?"

"Yes, that's correct."

"Well, then," continues Flob, "the fact that someone is doing something wrong is an entirely different sort of fact compared to the facts we can observe. Just like you, we *can* observe what is the case. We can observe that this man *is* stealing the purse. We can observe that the woman *is* upset. And so on."

I nod. So Flob continues.

"But the fact that the man down there is doing something wrong is clearly an extra fact on top of all these facts about what is the case. By saying that the man is doing something wrong you are clearly saying *more* than what he is doing. You are saying that he *should not be* doing what he is doing. So you are no longer just talking about what is the case."

I have to agree with Flob. The fact that the man is doing something wrong does seem to be an extra fact on top of all the other facts about what is the case.

"So you see," continues Flob, "we can observe only what is the case. And all of the facts about what is the case leave entirely open the question of whether that man *should* or *should not* be doing what he's doing. So please explain to us how you detect the extra fact that he *should not be* doing what he's doing. How do you detect the fact other that what he is doing is *wrong?*"

So how do I detect wrongness?
I look down. The man is still down there struggling to steal the woman's purse. I look at Flib and Flob. They raise their green eyebrows and look disappointed.

"I'm sorry," I say. "I just don't know *how* I detect the wrongness. I don't seem to be able to see it or feel it or taste it or smell it or touch it. But *somehow* I know it's out there."

The wrongness detector

A famous philosopher called G. E. Moore tried to solve the problem of explaining how we detect wrongness. He supposed that we have a sort of extra sense—a sixth sense—on top of our other five. We can't see, hear, smell, touch, or taste wrongness. But we can detect it, using this sixth sense. I shall call this extra sense our *wrongness detector*.

You might think of your wrongness detector as being a bit like an antenna. Just as sailors can use a radio antenna to detect a submarine hidden beneath the waves, so, too, does your wrongness detector allow you to detect the wrongness of what someone is doing despite the fact that you can't detect the wrongness with your other senses.

So I detect the wrongness of what the thief down in the street is doing by using my wrongness detector. Why can't Flib and Flob detect the wrongness of what the man is doing? Because they don't have a wrongness detector, of course.

Has Moore solved the problem of explaining how we detect wrongness? No. Not really. Moore has simply said that by some strange mechanism—a wrongness detector—we do manage to detect wrongness. But it remains utterly mysterious how this wrongness detector is supposed to work. So we are still left with a big mystery.

Back to where we started?

We have been examining the view that there are objective moral facts. On the view that there are objective moral facts, wrongness is "out there." It's a property that acts of stealing have, *anyway*, whatever anyone (including even God himself) might happen to think or feel about stealing.

We have also seen that there's a *big problem* with this view. If wrongness really were "out there," then it seems it would be a very *weird, undetectable* sort of property. In fact, it seems that if wrongness really were "out there," then we wouldn't be able to know about it.

So, as I can detect when someone is doing something wrong, it seems it can't be an objective fact that what they are doing is wrong.

A big advantage of the view that morality comes from us

It seems we are being forced back to where we started. We are back to the position that morality must *come from us* after all. For a really big advantage of the view that morality comes from us is that it very neatly explains why Flib and Flob can't detect the wrongness of what the robber is doing.

Take the Boo-Hooray Theory, for example. It clearly explains why Flib and Flob can't find the fact that makes what I say true when I say, "That man is doing something wrong!" According to the Boo-Hooray Theory, I am just *expressing* how I feel. It's as if I were shouting, "Boo to what that man is doing!" I don't make any claim at all. So what I say is *neither true nor false.*

But that means that Flib and Flob are on *a wild goose chase.* They are desperately looking for the "fact" that makes what I say "true."

But, of course, *there is no such fact.*

The Feelings Theory also neatly explains why Flib and Flob can't find the fact that makes what I say true. According to the Feelings Theory, when I say to Flib and Flob, "That man is doing something wrong!," what I say is true. What I say is made true by a fact. But, of course, what I say is not made true by an objective moral fact. It's not made true by a fact about how things are "out there" on the other side of the window. Rather, the fact that makes what I say true is a *fact about me*—the fact that I disapprove of what the man is doing.

That's why Flib and Flob can't find the fact that makes what I say true: they are looking in the wrong place. They're looking *out of the window.* In order to find the fact that makes what I say true, Flib and Flob must stop looking out of the window. They must turn around and examine *me.*

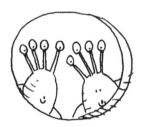

The big picture

We have taken quite a long and complicated philosophical journey. So you may now be feeling a bit lost. Let's take a step back to see where we've been. Let's get the big picture.

The big philosophical question we have been looking at is this: *Where does morality come from? Does morality come from us? Or does it come from God? Or are there objective moral facts?* That is, are things right or wrong *anyway*, independently of whatever we or God or anyone else might have to say about them?

In trying to answer this question, we have run up against a problem—a very famous philosophical problem. The problem is that we find ourselves being pulled in two directions at once. On the one hand, it seems that there must be objective moral facts. But, on the other hand, it seems that there *can't* be objective moral facts.

Why must there be objective moral facts? Because it seems that when we say "Killing is wrong," we make a claim made true by a fact—the fact that killing really is wrong. And this fact is an *objective fact*: killing must be wrong *anyway*, whatever we or the Vargs or even God might happen to think about killing. So even if we, the Vargs, and God all felt that killing was right . . .

. . . killing would still be wrong.

Why *can't* there be objective moral facts? Well, as Flib and Flob pointed out, if wrongness is "out there"—if wrongness is a property that killing has *anyway*, whatever anyone might happen to think about killing—then it seems we come up against an unsolvable mystery: how do we *detect* this property? It seems we *couldn't* detect it. In which case we couldn't know that killing is wrong. So, as we do know that killing is wrong, it seems it can't be an objective moral fact that killing is wrong.

How do we solve this puzzle? That is something that philosophers are still arguing about even today. I must admit, I am confused. I'm just not sure where morality comes from. What do you think?

Question 7

What is the mind?

My mind

This is me.

And this is a brick.

One important difference between me and the brick is this: unlike the brick, I have a mind.

So what goes on in my mind? Well, having a typical human mind means that I can *have experiences*. For example, I can enjoy the taste of marmalade and the smell of fresh coffee.

I can also *make decisions*. For example I can decide to go for a walk.

Having a typical human mind means I can also *feel sensations* like pain, and *work things out* (such as the answers to a crossword puzzle).

I can also *remember* things, *feel emotions* and *have beliefs* (such as my belief that it is going to rain).

A brick, on the other hand, can do none of these things.

Bat minds

It's not just human beings that have minds, of course. Take bats, for example. It seems that bats have minds, too. But it also seems that a bat's mind must be very different from our own.

Bats use something called *echolocation* to find their way about. The bat emits a very high-pitched, squeaking noise. This noise is so high-pitched that we humans cannot hear it.

This noise bounces back off the objects near the bat, producing an echo. The bat has very large, sensitive ears with which to hear this echo. The strength of the echo, the direction from which the echo comes, and the time it takes to return allow the bat to build up a picture of what's around it.

By using echolocation a bat can "see" even when it is pitch-dark. That's how bats can fly at night without bumping into anything.

I wonder what it must be like inside a bat's mind. How does the world seem to a bat when it "sees," using echolocation? The bat's experience must be very strange indeed. It seems it must be quite unlike any experience that we can have.

The brain

I don't just have a mind. I also have a brain. My brain is a rather gooey, gray-colored organ found in my head, right between my ears.

Atoms and molecules

The brain is of course a *physical object*. It's part of the physical universe. Just like every other physical object, my brain is made out of *physical matter*.

Physical matter is made up of tiny particles called *atoms*. These atoms group together to form slightly larger particles called *molecules*. Every physical object—be it your brain, a peanut, this piece of paper, a desk, or even planet Earth—is made out of atoms and molecules.

Cells

A living body is made out of tiny parts called cells.

Your body is made out of many billions of cells. The cells out of which your brain and nervous system are made are called *neurons*. This is a neuron.

There are about a *million million* neurons in your brain.

That's about as many neurons as there are stars in our galaxy! Each of these neurons is in turn made out of atoms and molecules.

How my mind and brain interact

What does the brain do? Some ancient Greeks thought the brain was simply an organ for cooling the blood (a bit like the way a car radiator cools water).

But, of course, nowadays we know that the brain has a different purpose. We know that the brain is closely connected to the mind. We know that what happens in the brain affects what happens in the mind, and that what happens in the mind affects what happens in the brain.

Many drugs illustrate how what happens in the brain can affect what happens in the mind.

For example, by subtly changing what's going on in my brain, a painkilling drug can make my experience of pain vanish.

Scientists have also discovered that by directly stimulating the brain in different ways, they can produce certain sorts of experience in the mind, such as visual experiences. For example, they have discovered that by applying a tiny electrical current to an area at the back of the brain, they can cause a person to experience a flash of light.

So there's no doubt that what happens in the brain can affect what happens in the mind. And the reverse is true, too. What happens in the mind can affect what happens in the brain.

For example, a scientist will tell you that when you decide to turn this page, something happens in your brain. Your brain sends electrical impulses down to the muscles in your arm. These impulses make the muscles move, making your hand turn the page . . .

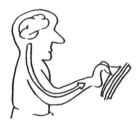

. . . like that. That movement of your arm was caused by something that happened in your brain.

So scientists have shown that the mind and the brain are closely connected. Still, most of what goes on inside the brain remains a mystery since it is incredibly complex. It is buzzing with chemical and electrical activity.

The mind is a private place

Here's a weird fact about minds: they seem to be *hidden* in a very peculiar way. Suppose I take a look at something bright purple— my bright purple pen, for example.

No one else can get inside my mind and have my experience of that color along with me. Only I can have my experience.

Of course, other people may have experiences that are *just like* mine. If you look at my pen, you will no doubt have a similar experience of its color. But your experience is yours, and my experience is mine.

In other words, it's as if my mind had a superstrong wall around it—a wall that prevents others from getting in.

All my experiences, thoughts, feelings, and so on are locked away behind this wall.

My mind seems to be like a secret garden, a hidden place within which only I can roam.

The inside of my mind seems to be hidden from others in a way that even the inside of my brain is not. Brain surgeons could X-ray my brain, of course.

They could even cut open my skull and look at what's going on in my brain. But it seems that not even a brain surgeon can get inside the realm of my mind. If they were to look inside my brain right now, they wouldn't come across my experience of the color of this pen. They wouldn't find anything bright purple. They would just find lots of gooey gray stuff.

Exactly the same is true of the mind of a bat. It seems quite impossible for us to get inside a bat's mind and find out what it's like to be a bat. It seems that even if we knew absolutely everything there is to know about what is going on physically inside a bat's brain when it "sees" an object using echolocation, that *still* wouldn't tell us what the experience is actually like for the bat, from inside its mind. We still wouldn't know what it's like to experience the world as a bat does.

The big question: what is the mind?

Let's now take a look at my philosophical question for this chapter. My question is, *What is the mind?* What is this thing that is conscious, that thinks, that enjoys experiences; that feels happiness, anger, and other emotions, that has hopes and fears; that makes decisions; and so on?

In this chapter we are going to look at two very different answers that philosophers have given to this question.

The first answer is that the mind is somehow *part of the physical world*. How could the mind be part of the physical world? Well, one obvious way would be if what goes on in your mind is just what goes on in your brain. Perhaps our thoughts, feelings, emotions, experiences, and so on are nothing more than certain physical processes taking place within our brains. Perhaps the mind just is the brain.

The second answer is that the mind is *separate from the physical world*. The mind may interact with the brain, but it is certainly not *the same thing* as the brain.

According to this second answer, our thoughts, feelings, emotions, experiences, and so on are *something extra*—something in addition to the buzz of activity going on in our brains.

Which of these two answers do you think is more plausible?

Aisha and Kobir

Remember Aisha? Well, she recently met Kobir, a friend of ours. Kobir is a science student. He studies at the university.

Aisha and Kobir decided to go for coffee in a local café. And, as you will soon discover, they ended up arguing about the mind. Kobir thought that the mind must be physical. But Aisha was convinced that the mind is something extra, something on top of what's going on physically.

KOBIR: Mmmm. I needed this.

AISHA: Me, too. I love coffee. So tell me, what have you been up to this morning?

KOBIR: This morning I went to one of Dr. Jones's lectures on the brain.

Aisha asked Kobir what that morning's lecture on the brain had been about.

KOBIR: Today Dr. Jones explained how all of our experiences of the world are caused by our sensory organs—our skin, eyes, nose, ears, and tongue—sending electrical impulses up to our brains.

AISHA: Really?

KOBIR: Yes. Here's an example. Take a sniff of this coffee. It smells good, doesn't it?

AISHA: Yes. It's great coffee.

KOBIR: Now, according to Dr. Jones, the experience you have as you smell this coffee is caused by tiny little particles traveling from the coffee up your nose.

These particles come into contact with cells on the inside of your nose.

Those cells then send electrical impulses up to your brain.

That causes something to happen in your brain. That's how you finally come to have that experience you're now having.

AISHA: How interesting!

KOBIR: Yes. It is, isn't it? It's fascinating to discover that all our experiences are really just something physical happening in our brains.

AISHA: What? Now just hold on a minute. You're getting a bit carried away!

Kobir looked surprised. Why was Aisha suddenly disagreeing with what he was saying?

KOBIR: What's the problem?

AISHA: Look, I know it's true that when I have this experience, something also happens in my brain.

KOBIR: Yes, that's right.

AISHA: But then you said that my experience is something physical happening in my brain, didn't you?

KOBIR: Of course.

AISHA: Well, I don't believe *that*! Science may have shown that when we have experiences, something also happens in our brains. In fact, it seems clear that our minds and our brains interact. But that doesn't prove that our experiences just are something happening in our brains, does it?

Why Aisha thinks her experience can't be in her brain

Aisha is surely right to say that while science may have shown that whenever something happens in our minds, something also happens in our brains, it doesn't follow that what happens in our minds just *is* what happens in our brains.

Still, is there any reason to suppose that Aisha's experience isn't something happening in her brain? Aisha thought there was.

> **Aisha:** Actually, I think it is pretty obvious that my experience *can't* be anything happening in my brain.
> **Kohir:** Why not?
> **Aisha:** Okay. Smell your coffee.

Aisha and Kobir both took a big sniff.

> **Aisha:** Now, what's your experience *like*?
> **Kobir:** What do you mean, what is it like?
> **Aisha:** Focus your attention on the experience. There's something that experience is like, isn't there? Something it's like *for you*, from *inside your mind*. So, tell me, *what* is it like?

Kobir took another sniff.

> **Kobir:** Mmmm. It's difficult to describe. It's very pleasant. Sort of *sharp and tangy*.
> **Aisha:** Yes, that's what mine's like, too.
> **Kobir:** So what's your point?

AISHA: Well, if you were to look inside my brain right now while I'm having this experience, you wouldn't find anything *sharp and tangy*, would you?

If you were to get inside my brain and examine it, you would just find lots of gooey gray brain stuff. No matter how closely you observed what's going on in my brain, nothing sharp and tangy would show up, would it?

KOBIR: I guess not.

AISHA: So, if my experience is sharp and tangy, but nothing in my brain is sharp and tangy, then my experience can't be anything in my brain, can it?

What do you think of Aisha's argument? Has Aisha shown that her experience isn't physical?

Do we have souls?

Kobir certainly wasn't convinced by Aisha's argument. In fact, he wasn't sure he understood what Aisha was suggesting.

KOBIR: I don't follow. So what *is* your experience, then, if it isn't physical? Surely, it *must* be physical. There is only the physical universe, after all.

But Aisha thought there had to be more than just the physical universe.

AISHA: I disagree. There's no way anything physical could have *this*, the sharp and tangy experience I'm having right now. There's no way it could actually *be conscious*. So, since I *do* have such experiences, since I *am* conscious, I can't be some physical thing, can I? I must be some other sort of thing.

KOBIR: What sort of thing?

AISHA: I must be a *soul*.

Now Kobir was really confused. He asked Aisha what she meant by a soul.

AISHA: A soul isn't part of the natural, physical universe that you scientists deal with. I'm not talking about a *physical* object, an object made out of *physical* matter, like a mountain, a lake, or a peanut. I'm talking about *some other sort of stuff entirely*. I'm talking about *nonphysical* stuff. *Supernatural* stuff. *Soul* stuff!

KOBIR: So you believe that you are not part of the physical universe? You—the thing that has conscious experiences, thoughts, and feelings, and so on—are a *soul*?

AISHA: Yes. That's right.

KOBIR: And I have a soul, too?

AISHA: Of course. We both have souls.

How does a soul experience smells?

Let's call Aisha's theory that each of us has a soul the *Soul Theory*.

164

According to Aisha, she has a physical body. But she herself is not something physical. She—the thing that has conscious experiences, that thinks and feels—is a soul. This means that after her physical body has died and no longer exists, Aisha can still carry on.

So how, according to the Soul Theory, does Aisha come to experience things in the physical world? How, for example, does Aisha come to experience the smell of the coffee in front of her?

Aisha agrees with Kobir that tiny particles from the coffee float up her nose. These particles then stimulate cells inside her nose— the cells that Kobir was talking about. The cells then send electrical impulses up to her brain.

But, according to Aisha, Kobir is wrong to say that what happens in Aisha's brain is her experience. It's her soul that has the experience, not her brain.

So how does Aisha's brain cause her soul to have the experience? Well, according to Aisha, it's as if her brain had a little transmitter. This transmitter allows her brain to send a message on to her soul.

That's how Aisha's soul comes to experience the smell of the coffee.

Heaven and reincarnation

Many religious people believe in the Soul Theory, of course. Some even believe that after their physical bodies die, their souls live. They go up to Heaven.

Others believe in *reincarnation*: they believe that when they die, their souls pass on to a new physical body (though it might be a nonhuman body—they could be reborn as a dog or a slug).

But though many people believe in the Soul Theory, it certainly is a lot to swallow. Even if you believe in the Soul Theory, you have to admit that the claim that there's not just physical stuff, there's also some sort of supernatural, soul stuff as well doesn't sound very scientific, does it?

A problem with the Soul Theory

Aisha got up and walked over to the dessert table. In front of her were two plates.

One plate had pieces of cake. The other had chocolate brownies. Aisha decided she wanted a chocolate brownie. So she put out her hand, put her fingers around one of the chocolate brownies, and picked it up.

Then Aisha sat down next to Kobir again and started munching on her brownie.

Kobir: Honestly, Aisha. There are no such things as souls. Souls are unscientific!

Aisha: Why?

Kobir: Look. Your body just moved. Your hand went out and picked up one of those chocolate brownies.

Aisha: Of course.

Kobir: Now, what *made* your hand move?

Aisha: Well, my hand was moved by the muscles in my arm. Those muscles were in turn moved by electrical impulses coming down from my brain.

Kobir: Yes. I agree. That is the scientific view. Your hand was made to move by *something that happened in your brain.*

Aisha: Yes.

Kobir: But I thought it was supposed to be your *soul* that made your hand move?

Aisha: It did. It made my hand move by making something happen in my brain. It's as if my brain had a little receiver that can receive messages sent from my soul.

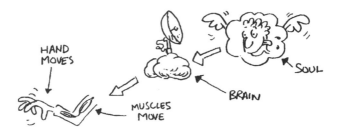

My soul made something happen in my brain. That made my muscles move. That made my hand grab the brownie.

KOBIR: So what happened in your brain was made to happen by your *soul*?

AISHA: Yes. Of course.

KOBIR: What happened in your brain wasn't made to happen by what's going on *physically*?

Aisha: No. Obviously not.

Kobir thought that he had now spotted a problem with Aisha's theory. He took a sip of coffee and started to explain the problem to Aisha.

KOBIR: I think I've discovered a problem with your theory, Aisha. The brain is part of the physical universe, isn't it?

AISHA: Of course.

KOBIR: Well, it seems that what happens in the physical universe is always fixed in advance by how things are physically.

AISHA: How do you mean?

KOBIR: Look. One minute before you picked up that brownie, you hadn't made any decision about whether to have a brownie or a piece of cake, had you?

AISHA: No. I hadn't even noticed the brownies or the cake.

KOBIR: Right. Yet it seems that if scientists knew absolutely everything there is to know about what was going on physically in this café one minute before you picked up that brownie. . . .

AISHA: Absolutely everything? Down to the movement of every last atom in my brain?

KOBIR: Yes, absolutely everything—if they did have *all* that information, then it would be possible for them to figure out that your hand would go out and pick up that brownie when it did.

You see, what happens in your brain, the movement of your hand—*all* these physical events are fixed in advance by how things are *physically*. Here's another example: the fact that our two bodies walked into this café this morning was fixed in advance by how things were physically two hours ago, even before we decided to come to the cafe.

AISHA: And so. . . ?

KOBIR: And so that means there's no possibility of something nonphysical like a soul affecting what happens at the physical level. That means *your soul won't be able to have any influence on what your body does.*

Aisha scratched her head and looked puzzled.

AISHA: Why not?

KOBIR: Look at it this way. Suppose that you had decided *not* to pick up a brownie. Suppose you had decided to pick up a piece of cake instead. Your hand would have picked up that chocolate brownie *anyway.*

It would pick up the brownie because it would be *made* to by how things are physically.

AISHA: Ah. I see. You are saying that when it comes to the physical universe, everything that happens is made to happen by how things were previously. So there's no room left for anything nonphysical to affect how things turn out. My soul won't be able to affect what my hand does.

KOBIR: That's right. So, if you *can* make your hand do what you want it to do, it seems you can't be a soul. The Soul Theory must be wrong.

AISHA: Oh, dear.

Kobir has just explained a very serious and very famous problem with the Soul Theory: if there were such things as souls, it seems they wouldn't be able to affect what our bodies do. Philosophers have tried a number of different ways of solving this problem. But I'm not sure any of their solutions really work. So perhaps, like Kobir, we should reject the Soul Theory.

A mystery

Someone who rejects the Soul Theory—who believes there's only *physical* stuff—is what's known as a *materialist*. According to materialists, there's just the natural, physical world. That means that I—the thing that has conscious experiences, that thinks, feels, and so on—must somehow be *part* of the physical universe.

170

Still, there is a great mystery facing materialism. The mystery is this: just how could part of the physical universe come to have the spark of consciousness? How could a mere lump of physical matter feel sadness or pain? How could it have this—the experience I have when I smell the cup of coffee on the desk in front of me? How, by simply bringing atoms and molecules together in a particular way, can one make *one of these: a mind*? That is what materialists like Kobir have to explain.

Kobir's theory

Actually, Kobir didn't think there really was that much of a mystery to solve here. He now started to explain to Aisha his theory about the mind.

> KOBIR: I think that each different type of mental state is actually just a type of *brain state*.
>
> AISHA: A brain state?
>
> KOBIR: Let me explain. The brain is a very complicated organ. It is made up of about a million million cells. These cells are called *neurons*. The neurons are woven together to form an incredibly complex web.

A BRAIN   NEURONS

> AISHA: But what have neurons got to do with consciousness? What have they got to do with my experience of pain, for example?
>
> KOBIR: Well, when someone is in pain, their brain is in a certain state. Certain neurons are firing in their brain.

AISHA: I see.

KOBIR: And it seems to me that for someone to be in pain *is just* the result of those neurons firing. Pain *just is* that particular brain state. The pain and the brain state are one and the same thing.

AISHA: I'm not sure I understand.

KOBIR: Look, often we discover that what we thought were two different things are actually *one and the same thing*, don't we? For example, an explorer might discover that the mountain he can see from a particular jungle and the mountain he can see from a particular desert are actually *one and the same mountain.*

The explorer hadn't realized up until that point that he had been looking at very same mountain but from two different sides.

AISHA: Ah! I see. You are saying that just as the mountain seen from the jungle turned out to be the very same mountain seen from the desert, so, too, may pain turn out to be a certain brain state. Pain and a brain state may also turn out to be one and the same thing.

KOBIR: Exactly!

AISHA: And the same goes for all our other conscious experiences, too?

KOBIR: Yes, that's right. The same goes for feeling happy, for experiencing the color yellow, for experiencing a bitter taste, and so on. Each of these different experiences is actually just a brain state.

AISHA: So this—the experience I'm having right now as I smell this coffee—is just a brain state?

KOBIR: Yes. That's right.

Let's call Kobir's theory that our experiences are really just brain states the *Brain Theory*.

"But the pain is in my foot. . . ."

You might have the following worry about the Brain Theory. Surely, you might think, When I feel a pain in my foot, the pain is located in my foot. So it isn't in my brain, is it?

Is this a good objection to the Brain Theory? Perhaps not. Here's one way of defending the Brain Theory against this objection. Sometimes, when people have had their legs amputated, it seems to them that they can still feel their legs. In fact, they often report feeling pain in their feet. But, of course, these people don't have feet any more. Their feet no longer exist.

In that case it can't be right to say that the pain these people feel is located in their feet. So where *is* their pain, then, if it isn't in

their feet? Well, these people wouldn't feel any pain if something wasn't happening in their brains, so an obvious suggestion to make is that their pain is in their brains. And if their pain is located in the brain, then presumably so is yours and mine.

Kobir's water example

Aisha now asked Kobir a question.

AISHA: Okay. If pain is a brain state—if to be in pain is just for certain neurons to be firing in the brain—then *which* brain state is it?

KOBIR: I have to admit, I don't know. We scientists haven't figured out which brain state pain is just yet. But there is every reason to suppose that we *will* find out one day.
Take a look at this glass of water. Being a scientist, I can tell you that water is H_2O. The glass is filled with molecules, each of which is made up of two atoms of hydrogen and one atom of oxygen, like this. . . .

Kobir sketched out this diagram on the back of a menu:

KOBIR: Scientists have shown that H_2O is just what water is. They have discovered that water and H_2O are *the very same thing.*

AISHA: What's this got to do with pain?

KOBIR: Well, I believe that one day scientists will similarly discover which state of the brain pain is. Perhaps they will do this by scanning the brains of people who are in pain.

I'm saying that just as water turned out to be H_2O, so, too, pain will turn out to be a certain brain state. Why not?

Kobir's Brain Theory certainly sounds very "scientific," doesn't it? In fact, many scientists think it pretty obvious that something like the Brain Theory must be true.

The Eyeless Alien Argument

Still, Aisha felt sure that the Brain Theory had to be wrong. It seemed obvious to her that her conscious experiences couldn't possibly turn out to be brain states. She now had one last attempt at explaining why.

AISHA: I'm afraid I still believe that your Brain Theory is false.

KOBIR: Why?

AISHA: I've already explained why. Brain scientists can enter into my brain. But they can never enter my mind. The mind is a *private place*, quite separate from the physical world.

KOBIR: I'm still not sure I understand your argument.

AISHA: Okay. Let me give you another example. I will *prove* to you that my experiences aren't anything physical.

KOBIR: Prove it? I doubt that!

AISHA: I accept your challenge! Let me tell you a story: the story of the *eyeless aliens*.

KOBIR: The eyeless aliens?

AISHA: Yes. Suppose that there are intelligent alien creatures who don't have eyes. They are completely blind.

KOBIR: So how do they find their way around?

AISHA: Mainly by touch—they have long wavy, tentacle-like arms—and by sound: they have big sensitive ears, just like bats do.

Now these aliens are also conscious, of course. They also have consious experiences. But, not having eyes, they don't have any experience of color. However, the aliens are very curious about us 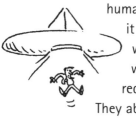 humans. In particular, they would like to know what it is like to be a human being, to experience the world as we do. They would *especially* like to know what it is like to experience color—to see the color red, for example. So what the aliens do is this. They abduct you.

They take you up in their flying saucer. They tie you up. Then they make you look at a number of different things they know we describe as red: a ketchup bottle, a strawberry, and so on.

KOBIR: Weird! Why do they do that?

AISHA: Well, when you look at these things, you have an experience of the color red. Then, while you are having that experience, the aliens scan your body, using an incredibly advanced scanner.

This scanner tells the *aliens absolutely* everything there is to know about what is going on inside you *physically* when you have that experience of red, including what is going on in your brain.

KOBIR: Absolutely everything? Down to the last atom?

AISHA: Yes. Absolutely everything. Now, here's the big question: will all this physical information about you tell the *aliens what it is actually like* to have an experience of red?

KOBIR: Hmmm. No. I guess not. They are blind. So they still won't know what it's *like* to see color.

AISHA: Exactly. It seems that, no matter how much information the aliens gather about what is going on inside you *physically* when you have the experience, including what is going on inside your brain, that still won't tell the aliens what the experience is *actually like* from the point of view of someone having it.

KOBIR: I see.

AISHA: So, here's my proof that the Brain Theory is false. The aliens *don't* know that you are experiencing *this*— what you and I experience when we look at that ketchup bottle. Right?

KOBIR: Right. I agree that they still don't know *that* fact.

AISHA: But their scanner does tell them all the *physical* facts about you, right?

KOBIR: Right.

AISHA: So, it follows that the fact that you are having that experience is not a *physical* fact about you! The experience itself is *nonphysical*!

KOBIR: But that can't be right.

AISHA: It is right!

KOBIR: No way! The experience must be something physical. There's just got to be something wrong with your argument!

AISHA: So what's wrong with it, then?

KOBIR: Er. I don't know.

The mystery of the mind

Let's now take a step back to see where we have got to. We have been looking at the question, *What is the mind?* Is the mind somehow part of the physical universe? Or is the mind something extra—

something that exists in *addition to* the physical? In trying to answer this question, we have found ourselves being pulled in two different directions at once.

Kobir has been pulling us in one direction.

He has an argument that seems to show our minds must some-how be part of the physical universe: it seems that, if our minds weren't physical, they wouldn't be able to make our bodies move about, which they can.

So why not just accept that our minds are physical, then? Because Aisha has an argument that pulls us in the other direction. Aisha's Eyeless Alien Argument seems to show that the facts about what goes on in our minds are hidden in a way that the *physical* facts about us are not. In that case it seems that the mind can't be physical.

So it seems that the mind has to be part of the physical world. Yet on the other hand, it seems it can't be part of the physical world. So which is it? I have to admit, I'm not sure. And I'm not the only one. Today, at universities all over the world, philosophers and scientists continue to struggle with the question of how our minds and our physical bodies are related.

What do you think?

Question 8

Does God exist?

The universe

I am sitting on top of a hill under a beautiful night sky.

The stars are twinkling brightly. To the east of me, the moon sits above the treetops, almost full. To the west, I can see the spires of Oxford. Above the spires there is a faint purple glow where the sun set just a few minutes ago. Between the glow and the moon are suspended two bright points of light—the planets Venus and Jupiter.

As I sit here on this hilltop, I am struck by how vast the universe is. Here we are, sitting on the cool outer crust of a huge ball of red-hot rock: planet Earth.

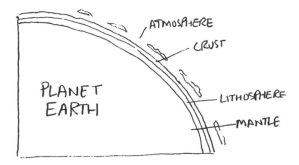

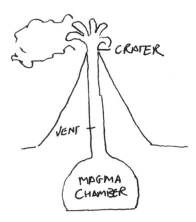

Every now and then a little molten rock—lava—spurts out to form a volcano.

Earth turns on its axis once every twenty-four hours. That is what made the sun disappear from view a little while ago, of course: it was not the sun that moved, but Earth that turned. The moon—another big ball of rock—goes round Earth once a month.

And Earth goes around the sun once a year.

Those two bright points of light over there—Venus and Jupiter—are also planets. In fact, there are nine planets in our solar system, all of them rotating slowly around the sun.

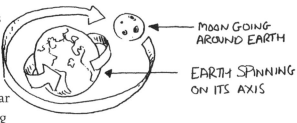

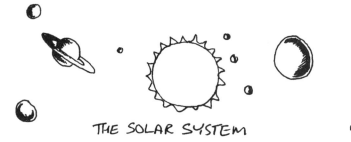

THE SOLAR SYSTEM

Our sun is a star just like the thousands of other stars that I can see up above me. Those other stars are much further away, of course. While light from the sun takes just eight minutes to reach us, light from other stars can take tens, hundreds, or even thousands of years.

The stars I see spread out above me form part of a huge whirlpool of stars called a *galaxy*. Our galaxy is called the *Milky Way*,

the Milky Way being just one of the thousands of known galaxies in the universe.

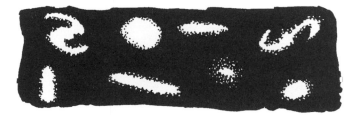

Against this vast universe, planet Earth seems almost unimaginably tiny and insignificant.

Where did the universe come from?

When I look out across the universe, I often ask myself: How did all this rock and dust and space come to be here? Where did it all come from? What *made* it exist? Scientists have a theory about this. They say that the universe began with a huge explosion. Scientists call this explosion the *Big Bang*.

The Big Bang happened a very long time ago—between ten and twenty thousand million years ago. The Big Bang was where all the matter in the universe came from. It was the beginning of space. In fact, it was the beginning of time itself.

But when scientists tell me this, it doesn't help me very much. It doesn't remove my feeling that something still needs explaining. Because I then want to know: *What made the Big Bang happen?* Why was there a bang, rather than no bang? That certainly is a great mystery, perhaps the greatest mystery of all.

The meaning of life

After a while, I stop looking up at the universe spread out above me. I look down at the grass.

I notice that, down in the shadows among the blades of grass, tiny insects are crawling about. Many of these insects are ants. They seem to be very busy. When I look even more closely, I see that the ants are pushing a leaf around.

It seems that ants are trying to push the leaf into a hole in the ground. That hole must be where the ants live. The leaf can hardly fit. The ants struggle and struggle and still they can't get it into the hole. I wonder why the leaf is so important to them.

I could easily put my foot down and squash all the ants. I decide not to squash them. But I wonder what real difference it would make if I did. Look at their frantic activity, running around, trying to get that leaf into the hole. It all seems so pointless. So meaningless. What would it really matter if I did put my foot down and snuff them out?

Looked at from space, Earth must seem a bit like a huge ants' nest.

There we all are, rushing about, just like ants. We are born. We grow up. We go to the supermarket. We go to work. We watch TV. We have children. We die. Our children have children, who in turn have children. Generation after generation of ceaseless activity. On and on the cycle goes. But what is the meaning behind our brief journey through life? What is the point of our being momentarily alive and conscious on this tiny planet amid all this vastness? Is there any point?

God

As I sit here under the stars, I have been puzzling about the existence of the universe. Why is it here? What made the Big Bang happen? Why was there a bang, rather than no bang? I have also been wondering about the meaning of life. What is the point of our being here?

Many people would answer the question about what caused the universe to exist by saying that God did: God created the universe. God made the Big Bang happen.

Many people also believe that it is God who gives meaning to our existence. They believe that there is a point to our being here. We do have a purpose, a divine purpose. That purpose involves loving and obeying God.

What is God like?

If God did create the universe, if He is what gives meaning to our lives, then what is He like? Some people think of God as being a bit like this:

But of course, this can't be quite right. God isn't really an old man with a big beard. He doesn't *really* sit on a cloud. If you were to fly about and examine all the clouds that there are, you wouldn't find an old man sitting on any of them. Rather, this is just an image that religious people use to help them think about God.

In fact, although I talk about God as being a He, many people nowadays don't even think of God as being male.

So what is God like, then, if He isn't an old man sitting on a cloud? According to Christians, Jews, Muslims, and those of many other religious faiths, God has at least the following three characteristics:

First of all, God is *all powerful*. That means He can do absolutely anything. He created the universe. And He could destroy it again, if He so chose. God can bring the dead back to life, turn water into wind, and send you to the moon in the blink of an eye.

Second, God is supposed to be *all knowing*. God knows everything there is to know. He knows all that has happened, and all that will happen. He knows our thoughts. He knows our every secret. He even knows that it was I who sneaked downstairs last night and stole the last piece of cake from the fridge.

Absolutely nothing is hidden from God.

Third, God, is supposed to be *all good*. God loves us and would certainly never do anything bad.

Why believe in God?

Of course, many religious people have *faith* in the existence of God. They believe in God's existence without reason. They just believe.

But, as philosophers, we are interested in whether there is any *reason* to believe in the existence of God. Is there any evidence to suggest that God exists? Can we show by argument that God exists? Or is there perhaps some reason to suppose that God doesn't exist? These are the questions we are going to look at here.

Bob and Kobir arrive

I lie back in the grass and look up at the stars. After a while I hear two voices in the distance. They seem to be getting nearer. Eventually, I recognize who it is. It's Bob and Kobir out for an evening stroll (you remember Kobir—he was the science student from the last chapter).

Bob is a soccer player. He's staying with Kobir for the weekend. The two of them have been kicking a ball around in the park.

A couple of minutes later they arrive on top of the hill. We all say hello, and lie down on the grass.

I explain to Bob and Kobir that I have been thinking about God, the Big Bang, and the meaning of life.

They are pretty impressed! Bob says that he believes in God. Kobir, on the other hand, says he doesn't.

Now, Bob and Kobir are good friends. But there's nothing they enjoy more than having a philosophical argument. So it isn't long before they are busy arguing about whether or not God exists. This is how the argument starts.

Bob: Look. You have to admit, many millions of people all over the earth believe in God. If all those millions believe, then there's got to be *something* to it, doesn't there?

Kobir: I'm afraid that's wrong. Millions of people used to believe that the earth was flat and that the sun went around the earth. They were quite wrong about *that*, weren't they?

Bob: Well, okay. I admit they were wrong about that.

Kobir: So you see, most people *can* be wrong. Just because many or even most people believe in God doesn't show that He exists.

Bob: Okay. I suppose it's true that most people *can* be wrong. But it's *likely* that they're right isn't it?

KOBIR: No. Not if they don't have *reason* to believe. And of course, the explanation of why people believe things is not always that they have reason to believe. Sometimes there's another explanation.

BOB: Like what?

KOBIR: Well, many of those who believe in God are simply *brought up* to have that belief. Belief in God is often drilled into people from a very young age.

That explains why they believe.

BOB: That doesn't explain why I believe in God. I was never sent to Sunday school. And neither of my parents believes in God.

KOBIR: I would also say that many people believe in God, not because they have any reason to believe that God exists, but just because they *want* to believe He exists. They believe in God simply because it is a nice, comforting thing to believe.

BOB: Why comforting?

KOBIR: Well, it's a scary thought that we are all alone in the universe, that there is no ultimate meaning or point to our existence. It's quite frightening to think that when we die, we are gone forever. It is so much *nicer* to believe that there is a loving God who watches over us and who gives some point to our lives. It is so much *nicer* to believe that when we die, we don't just cease to exist, but continue on. But just because this is a nice, comforting thing to believe doesn't give us the slightest reason to suppose that it's *true*, does it?

Is Kobir being entirely fair? Actually, in some ways believing in God can make life seem rather less comfortable. For example, some people who believe in God also believe in the Last Judgment and Heaven and Hell. They believe that after they die they will be judged by God and possibly sent to Hell as punishment for the bad things they have done.

That's hardly a very comforting thought, is it?

Still, it appears that most people who believe that God exists do also want it to be true that He exists. It seems they get quite a lot of comfort from their belief. So is Kobir right? Do most people believe in God simply because they want to believe or have been brought up to believe in God? Or is there also some reason to suppose that God exists? What do you think?

Bob's Big Bang Argument

The three of us sit up silently for a few minutes.

We listen to the sound the wind makes as it hisses through the trees down at the bottom of the hill.

Suddenly, there is a whooshing sound followed by a deafening bang. It's the sound of a firework. It showers the sky to the north of us with thousands of silver flecks. We watch as they spiral downward.

Bob: Look. I certainly *don't* believe God exists just because it's a *nice* thing to believe. After all, I'd like to believe that fairies exist, but I don't. There's no *reason* to believe in them. There's no evidence that they exist. But there *is* evidence that God exists. That's why I believe in God.

Kobir: What do you mean? What evidence is there that God exists?

Bob: Well, Stephen mentioned the Big Bang a minute ago. Don't scientists believe that the universe we see spread out up there began with a huge explosion—the Big Bang?

Kobir: Yes.

Bob: Well then, my question is, What caused the Big Bang? Why was there a bang rather than no bang?

Kobir: I have no idea. That is a mystery.

Bob: Yes, it's a great mystery After all, everything has a cause, doesn't it? Things don't *just happen*. Take that firework that exploded over there a few moments ago. That explosion didn't *just happen*, did it? It had to have a cause. People had to light the fuse, didn't they?

Kobir: I guess so.

Bob: But then the same applies to the Big Bang. The Big Bang must have had a cause, too. Now if God exists, that would solve the mystery of what caused the Big Bang. That's why it's reasonable to suppose that God exists. God explains why the Big Bang happened. God lit the fuse!

Is Bob's Big Bang Argument any good?

I think that often, when it seems to people that God must exist, something like Bob's Big Bang Argument is at the back of their minds. Indeed, you can find much the same sort of argument in the writings of many philosophers and religious thinkers down through the centuries.

At first sight, Bob's Big Bang Argument does seem quite convincing. But is it really any good? Does Bob's argument actually provide us with some reason to suppose that God exists?

Kobir certainly doesn't think so.

KOBIR: I'm afraid your argument is no good. You haven't given us any reason at all to assume that God exists.

BOB: Why not? Look, in a nutshell your argument is this: everything has a cause; therefore the universe has a cause; therefore God must exist as the cause of the universe. Right?

KOBIR: Yes. I guess so.

BOB: Well then, if *everything* has a cause, then what caused God? What made Him exist?

KOBIR: Good question. That's a mystery.

BOB: So you have merely replaced one mystery with another, haven't you?

KOBIR: How do you mean?

BOB: Well, we are still stuck with a mystery, aren't we? We started with the question, What caused the universe?

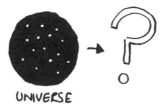

UNIVERSE

Scientists give us the answer: the Big Bang. But then we are left with a mystery, aren't we? For then there is the mystery of what caused the Big Bang.

Now you try to get rid of *this* mystery by saying that God caused the Big Bang. But then we face the mystery of what caused God.

And so on. There's still a mystery left over.

Kobir is right. Bob suggested that it is reasonable to believe that God exists because that solves a mystery—the mystery of why the Big Bang happened. The trouble is, Bob has removed one mystery only by introducing another. Still, Bob doesn't give up that easily.

BOB: Okay. Let's suppose God doesn't have a cause. Let's suppose God isn't the sort of thing that needs a cause. If God doesn't need a cause, then there's no mystery left over.

KOBIR: But now you have contradicted yourself! You started your argument by assuming that *everything* has a cause. Now you are saying not everything has a cause—God doesn't.

BOB: But when I said everything has a cause, I didn't mean absolutely everything. I meant everything except God, obviously.

KOBIR: So you are saying there is one exception to the rule that everything has a cause: God.

Bob: Yes. God is the exception to that rule.

Kobir: But if there has to be an exception to the rule, why not just make the universe the exception to the rule instead? What reason have you given us to add God on to the beginning of the universe as an *extra* cause? You have given us no reason. But then you have given us no reason to assume that God exists.

Bob: I guess you're right.

Kobir: You see, Bob, I admit that there *is* a mystery about where the universe came from. I admit that it is a great mystery why there is something rather than nothing. I just deny that this mystery gives us any reason at all to suppose that God exists.

Bob's Cosmic Watchmaker Argument

Bob sits up. He starts fiddling with his watch. Bob is clearly a bit upset that his Big Bang Argument doesn't work after all. Eventually, after a few minutes, Bob takes another shot at convincing Kobir of the existence of God. He takes off his watch and tosses it on to the grass in front of Kobir.

Bob: Okay, Kobir. Here's a better argument. Take a look at this watch. Suppose that you are walking along a deserted beach on a remote island somewhere. Suddenly, you come across a watch just like this one. It's just lying there on the sand.

You ask yourself: how did the watch get here? Here are two suggestions. The first suggestion is that the watch was *designed*. It's a tool, made by an intelligent being—a watchmaker—for a specific purpose—to enable people to tell the time. The second suggestion is that the watch was made by the action of the waves, the wind, and other natural forces. They formed the watch all by themselves, without the help of any sort of designer. Which of these two suggestions is more likely to be true, do you think?

KOBIR: Well, obviously, the first suggestion is much more likely to be true.

BOB: You're right. A watch is not like a pebble, is it? Pebbles are formed without help from any intelligence. They really are formed by natural forces: the wind and the waves. But a watch is hardly likely to have been made in this way, right?

KOBIR: No.

BOB: In fact, the watch clearly has a purpose—to tell the time. So isn't it reasonable to suppose that there must be an intelligent being who designed it for that purpose? There must be a designer, a watchmaker, who made it.

KOBIR: I agree.

BOB: Now take a look at my eye.

The eye is a very complicated object—far, far more complicated than a watch or anything we human beings can make. Like the watch, the eye also has a purpose—to enable the creature attached to it to see. It does this job extremely well, doesn't it?

Kobir: Yes, it does. The eye is a marvelous piece of engineering.

Bob: Now ask yourself: how did the eye come to exist? What is more likely—that the eye came into existence by chance or that it was designed? Given that the eye has a purpose, a purpose for which it is very well suited, it, too, must have a designer. There has to be a designer—a sort of cosmic watchmaker—who designed the eye. That designer is God.

Is there a problem with Bob's Cosmic Watchmaker Argument?

What do you think of Bob's Cosmic Watchmaker Argument? As happened to the Big Bang Argument, different versions of it have been put forward down through the centuries by philosophers and religious thinkers. But there are problems with it.

One problem with the Cosmic Watchmaker Argument is that nowadays we know all about *natural selection*. Natural selection can explain how eyes might come to exist without supposing they had any sort of a designer.

Natural selection

Here's how natural selection works. When someone is going to build something complex like a ship, airplane, or building, they usually make a plan. This plan is called a *blueprint*. The blueprint shows exactly how the ship or whatever is to be put together.

Now, all living things also contain a sort of blueprint. They contain something called *DNA*.

DNA

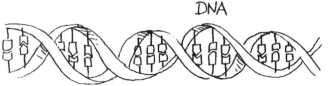

194

DNA is a long string of molecules. You will find one of these strings in every cell of a living thing's body. The string contains a blueprint for making a living thing of that sort. When plants or creatures reproduce, it is the string of DNA handed down from the parent plants or creatures that provides the blueprint for building it.

The DNA string in the new living thing is made by copying parts of the DNA string from the parent or parents. But in the process of copying, slight errors may creep in.

Because of these slight changes to the blueprint, the creature produced from it may be slightly different from its parent or parents. There will be slight changes to the creature. These changes are called *mutations*. They happen quite by chance.

Here's an example. A simple creature living in the sea may have, as a mutation, a single light-sensitive cell on its skin.

Now, this cell could be very useful to the creature. It may allow it to detect how deep it is in the sea (the deeper you go in the sea, the darker it gets). So in this environment the mutation would give the creature a slight advantage over other creatures of that sort.

Another one of these creatures may have as a mutation a brighter-colored skin. This mutation may be a big disadvantage to the creature in that environment, making it more visible to other creatures that want to eat it.

Of course, the creature with the mutation that helps it to survive is more likely to be able to mate and reproduce itself than a creature with a mutation that makes it less likely to survive. So the next generation of creatures is more likely to contain creatures with the light-sensitive cell and is less likely to contain creatures with the brightly colored skin. Those mutations which help creatures survive and reproduce in that environment are likely to be passed on and those which make survival less probable are wiped out.

As further mutations are added over thousands and thousands of generations, the creatures slowly change. They gradually *evolve*. They adapt to their environments. The process is called *natural selection*.

You have probably come across fossils—pieces of rock that have taken on the form of living creatures that lived millions of years ago. When you look at fossils, you can see the kinds of change that I have been talking about taking place. For example, it seems that the first birds to exist actually evolved from certain sorts of dinosaur.

We have even traced parts of our own evolutionary tree. We now know that human beings share a common ancestor with apes. It is no accident that we look so similar to them.

So how did the *eye* appear? It didn't just appear from anywhere. It evolved over millions and millions of years. It evolved because it helps creatures to survive and reproduce. Perhaps the process began with a single light-sensitive cell appearing in some simple organism living in the sea. Gradually, over many generations, more light-sensitive cells were added. In this way, the eye slowly began to evolve, until finally you see the sort of eye that is around today.

So one big problem with Bob's Cosmic Watchmaker Argument is this. Before we knew about natural selection, it seemed difficult to explain how eyes, and living creatures generally, could come to exist on the earth. We couldn't see how any *natural* process could have produced complex living creatures. For this reason, many people supposed that there must be a *supernatural* being—God— who made the creatures. But now that we know about evolution and natural selection, this particular reason for believing in the existence of God has disappeared.

We don't know the *whole* story of how life on earth developed, of course. I am just guessing about how the eye might have evolved. The point is that we can see that, in principle, the existence of all the different sorts of life on earth can very probably be explained in wholly natural terms without our having to talk about God at all.

What is reasonable to believe?

Kobir explains natural selection to Bob. After he's explained, Bob admits that the eye does not seem to provide much evidence after all for the existence of God.

I'm now feeling pretty hungry. Bob and Kobir say that they are hungry, too, so we decide to go for curry at my favorite Indian restaurant. We get up, dust ourselves off, and start off down the hill. There's a gravel path which crunches underfoot. The moon lights our way, casting long shadows out in front of us.

As we walk downhill, Kobir tells Bob that he doesn't think there are *any* good arguments for the existence of God. There's no proof of the existence of God. There is little if any evidence to suggest that God exists.

Bob tosses his soccer ball in the air a few times. Then he points out, quite correctly, that even if there is no good reason to suppose God does exist, that doesn't prove He doesn't exist. Kobir agrees that this is true.

> **BOB:** But, then, shouldn't we remain *neutral* about whether or not God exists? I mean, if we can't show He does exist, but can't show He doesn't exist either, isn't remaining neutral the most reasonable view to take?
>
> **KOBIR:** Actually, I don't so. I think that if there is no reason to suppose exists, then the reasonable thing to believe is that He *doesn't* exist.

Another firework explodes above us. We stand and watch for a moment as it sends shimmering red sparks across the sky.

Bob: But why? Look, think about the question of whether or not there is life out there in other parts of the universe. It seems that at the moment we can't show that there definitely is life out there, but neither can we show that there isn't. In which case, the most reasonable position to take is to remain neutral.

Kobir: I agree. I think we should remain neutral on whether there is life out there. But the question of whether or not God exists is different.

Bob: Why?

Kobir: Because while there is little if any reason to suppose God exists, there *is* some good evidence that there must be alien life-forms.

Bob: What evidence? We haven't discovered life on other planets.

Kobir: True. But we know that life evolved here on this planet, don't we? And we also know there are countless millions of other planets in the universe, many of which are very similar to our own. In which case it seems not improbable that life will have evolved on at least one of those other planets, too. So there *is* pretty good evidence for the existence of life out there. It's just that we don't have conclusive

ALIEN LIFE-FORMS

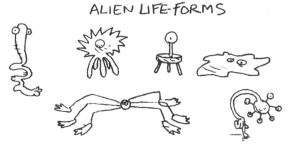

evidence. On the other hand, it seems to me that there is little if any evidence to suggest that God exists.

Bob shrugs his shoulders. He doesn't look convinced. So Kobir continues.

Kobir: Look. Compare believing in fairies. If there's little if any reason to suppose that fairies exist, then it is probably more reasonable to believe that they *don't* exist rather than to remain neutral. Don't you agree?

Bob: I suppose so. I certainly believe that fairies don't exist. It's silly to believe in fairies.

Kobir: Well, then. The same is true of God. If there is little or no reason to believe that God exists, then the reasonable thing to believe is that He doesn't exist. Isn't it as silly to believe in God as it is to believe in fairies?

Bob feels quite insulted by Kobir's comparing belief in God to belief in fairies. And perhaps Kobir is being a bit unfair. After all, plenty of very intelligent people believe in God. And, surely, believing in God is certainly not silly in the sense that it is frivolous or trivial: believing in God can have huge, life-changing consequences.

Still, the question remains: is there any more reason to believe in God than there is to believe in fairies? If Kobir is right, there isn't. But then isn't it more reasonable to believe that God *doesn't* exist, rather than to remain neutral on whether or not He exists? What do you think?

The problem of suffering

As we near the bottom of the hill, a large shadowy shape starts to loom up in front of us. It's the local hospital. Many of the windows are lit. Through some of the windows we can see figures moving around. At one window quite near to us, we notice a woman. She looks sad, as if she has been crying.

200

As we walk past the hospital, Kobir starts to explain why he thinks that, actually, there is very good evidence to suggest that God *doesn't* exist.

> KOBIR: I think you should agree, Bob, that if there's no reason to suppose God does exist, then the reasonable view to take is that He doesn't. But in any case, we have all been overlooking something. You keep suggesting that there is no reason to suppose that God doesn't exist. But, actually, there is.
>
> BOB: What do you mean? What evidence is there that God *doesn't* exist?

Kobir stops and points at the hospital.

> KOBIR: *There's* my evidence. God is supposed to have at least three characteristics, isn't he? Isn't He supposed to be all powerful, all knowing, and all good?
>
> BOB: That's right.
>
> KOBIR: Well now, there is a great deal of pain and suffering in the world, isn't there? People get horrible diseases. Many of the people in that hospital right now are suffering from terrible, painful diseases. There are also wars. Famines. Earthquakes. You have to admit that in many ways the world is not a very nice place in which to be. It seems it could definitely be nicer.

> BOB: That's true. It could be nicer.

KOBIR: The problem is, if God has these three characteristics—if He really is all powerful, all knowing, and all good—then *why* is there pain and suffering in the world? Why isn't the world nicer?

BOB: I don't really see the problem.

KOBIR: Well, if God is all powerful—if He can do anything—then he can stop the pain and suffering, can't He?

BOB: Yes. I guess He could.

KOBIR: In fact, he could have made the world so that it contained no pain and suffering in the first place, couldn't He? He could have made it so that we couldn't feel the sensation of pain, for example. He could have made a world free of disease. He could have made a much more pleasant world for us. In fact, He could have made the earth like Heaven is supposed to be. But he didn't. So *why* didn't he?

BOB: I don't know. Maybe he didn't realize how things would turn out.

KOBIR: But He *must* have realized. God is supposed to be all knowing. He knows everything, including how things will turn out. In which case it seems that God makes us suffer *on purpose*!

BOB: But God would never do that! God is good. He would never make us suffer on purpose.

KOBIR: There's the problem. Either God isn't all powerful, or God isn't all knowing, or God isn't all good. But God, if He exists, has all three of these characteristics. Therefore God doesn't exist!

This is a very old, very famous, and very serious problem facing those who believe in God. Religious thinkers have been struggling with the problem for a very long time. Let's call it the *Problem of Suffering*. Can the problem be solved?

The Free-Will answer

The three of us think about the Problem of Suffering as we continue to walk. Some people who believe in God have tried to deal with the Problem of Suffering by arguing that responsibility for the pain and suffering in the world lies not with God but with us. And in fact this is precisely what Bob now suggests.

> **Bob:** You are forgetting something. God gave us *free will.*
> **Kobir:** How do you mean?
> **Bob:** God gave us the ability to *choose for ourselves* how we will act. Without free will, we would be just like machines or robots. We'd simply be made to act in the way we do. We couldn't do otherwise. But we can choose to do otherwise. For example, we chose to walk up this hill this evening. But we could just as easily have chosen to go to the movies instead.
> **Kobir:** How does free will help you solve the problem about suffering?
> Bob: Well, unfortunately we often choose to do things that result in pain and suffering. We start wars, for example. Now God can't be held responsible for a war, can He? The suffering caused by our wars is *our* fault, not His.

> **Kobir:** But wouldn't it have been better if God hadn't given us free will? Wouldn't it have been better if he had just *made us* so we always do the right thing? Then there wouldn't be any pain or suffering. There wouldn't be any wars.
> **Bob:** No, because then we would be mere puppets, mere robots, wouldn't we? It is much better that we have free will, despite the fact that we do sometimes end up causing suffering.

A problem with the Free-Will answer

Let's call Bob's answer to the Problem of Suffering the Free-Will answer. The Free-Will answer is quite ingenious.

However, there are big problems with it. As Kobir points out, one of the most obvious problems with the Free Will Answer is that it seems much of the pain and suffering in the world isn't caused by us.

> KOBIR: The trouble with your argument is that not all of the suffering in the world is our fault. Okay, we cause wars. But what about a horrible disease? What about a disease like cancer which kills millions of people every year in a very unpleasant way. How is that disease *our* fault? How did *we* cause it? Or take a flood.

> A flood may drown many thousands of people. How can that be *our* fault? It seems it can't be. But then there can be no God.

Bob throws his soccer ball in the air a few times while he thinks for a moment.

> BOB: Maybe the disease and the flood *are* caused by us. It's just that we don't *realize* that we caused them.
>
> KOBIR: How do you mean?
>
> BOB: Well, for example, maybe the flood was indirectly caused by our cutting down the rain forests, causing the weather to change a lot. That caused a

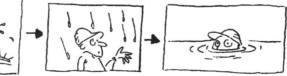

heavy rain to fall, which in turn caused the flood.

KOBIR: Maybe. But it's very hard to believe that the pain and suffering in the world is somehow caused by us, isn't it? How do we make earthquakes happen, for example? It's certainly very hard to believe that, if only *we* were to act in certain ways, then there would never be *any* pain or suffering at all!

BOB: I guess you are right. I guess God, if He exists, must be responsible for at least *some* of our suffering.

Is suffering God's punishment?

Bob has one last stab at dealing with the Problem of Suffering.

BOB: Maybe the suffering that God causes is intended as a *punishment.*

KOBIR: A punishment for what?

BOB: For our sins. For the wrongs we have done. God is good. He loves us. But just as good and loving parents must sometimes punish their children when they do something wrong, so, too, must God sometimes punish us.

Bob's suggestion makes Kobir rather angry.

KOBIR: Honestly, that really is a terrible suggestion!

BOB: Why is it terrible?

KOBIR: Look. Many of the disasters that occur happen to people who can't be blamed for anything at all. Very young babies, for example. Even if *we* have done something wrong, *they* haven't done anything wrong, have they?

BOB: I guess not.

KOBIR: So why is it fair to punish *them*? Suppose our law courts were to punish the babies of adults who had committed crimes?

That would hardly be fair, right? In fact, that would be a pretty *horrible* thing to do, wouldn't it?

BOB: I guess so.

KOBIR: Right. So why is it any less horrible if God punishes the babies of adults who have done wrong? A good God would never do such a cruel and despicable thing.

Bob and Kobir have been talking about the *Problem of Suffering*. The problem is, if God is all good, all knowing, and all powerful, then why is there so much suffering in the world? As you can see, this is a very serious problem for those who believe in God. Bob hasn't really managed to solve the problem. Can you think of a better solution?

Faith

The three of us finally arrive at the restaurant and go inside.

I'm now very hungry, so I order a huge plate of poppadoms for us to nibble on while we make up our minds about what curry to order. In between nibbling on his poppadom, Bob makes a very interesting point about believing in God.

BOB: Okay. Suppose I accept that there's little if any evidence that God exists. Suppose I accept there's no good reason to suppose He exists. Suppose I accept there's even some evidence to suggest that God doesn't exist. Still, this is all irrelevant when it comes to my belief in God.

KOBIR: Why?

BOB: Because when it comes to believing in God, it's not a question of believing for a *reason*. *Reason* has nothing to do with it. Belief in God is a matter of *faith*. You must *just believe.* Many people have faith in the existence of God. And faith is a very positive thing to have, don't you agree?

Is Bob right? Is faith in God's existence a good thing to have?

It is worth remembering that faith can sometimes be a dangerous thing. For example, faith can be used to control people. Once people have let go of reason, once they just believe, then they are easily controlled. The unscrupulous leader of a religion can take advantage of a simple, trusting faith and use it to his or her own advantage.

Faith, taken to an extreme, also makes it difficult to communicate with people. One can no longer reason or argue with them. If people with an extreme faith get it into their heads that they should do some terrible thing (perhaps kill those with religious beliefs different from their own), it may be impossible to make them see that what they are doing is wrong. They won't listen to reason.

On the other hand, there is no doubt that faith in the existence of God can have a positive effect. It can and does help many people. If you trust in the existence of a good God, that may help you to deal with some of the bad things that happen to you in life.

It is also true that faith in the existence of God has transformed some people's lives for the better. Rather than being selfish and cruel, they have become generous and noble.

BEFORE   AFTER

Religious faith has even led people to lay down their lives to save others (though we should remember that it is not only those who believe in God that do such noble and unselfish things). So there are good things about having faith in the existence of God.

What does it all mean?

For those who have religious faith, life does have meaning. We are here for a purpose: God's purpose. Many believe that this purpose is to love and obey God. But what if you don't have faith? What if you don't believe there is a God? What is one to say about the meaning of life then? If there is no God, then is life meaningless?

If there is no God, then perhaps it is up to us to give life its meaning. The purpose our lives have is the purpose that we give to them. If that is true, then we each have a big responsibility. You can choose to live a meaningless life, or a meaningful one. What sort of life you live is up to you.

Philosophical Jargon

APARTHEID A system in which people of different races are segregated, usually because one race is felt to be superior to another. There was an apartheid system in South Africa until quite recently.

ATOM A very, very small particle (though there are particles that are even smaller, particles out of which atoms are themselves made). Atoms group together to form molecules. For example, a molecule of water is made up of two atoms of hydrogen and one of oxygen. Atoms are what all physical objects (like peanuts, chairs, mountains, and galaxies) are made up of.

BIG BANG The huge explosion which scientists suppose began the formation of the physical universe.

CELL All living things are made up of tiny parts called cells. For example, your body is made out of many billions of cells. All cells are in turn made out of atoms and molecules.

COMMON SENSE What most of us take to be obvious.

EVIDENCE Evidence is information that supports a belief. For example, suppose I believe there is someone living in that cottage over there. . . .

The information that there is smoke coming out of the chimney supports my belief, makes it more likely that my belief is true.

EVOLUTION Species 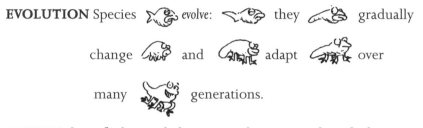 evolve: they gradually change and adapt over many generations.

FAITH To have faith is to believe something, even though there may be little if any reason to believe it.

GALAXY A huge cluster of stars. There are millions and millions of stars in our galaxy, the Milky Way.

GOD The supreme being who is supposed to be all powerful, all knowing, and all good.

HEAVEN The wonderful, supernatural place to which, according to many religions, we go to when we die (at least, we do if we have been good).

KNOWLEDGE Just because you believe something doesn't mean that you know it. Your belief has got to be true. But even that isn't enough. Many philosophers would say that in order for a true belief to count as knowledge, you must also have some reason to suppose your belief is true.

MATERIALISM The theory that there is only physical matter—matter made out of atoms and molecules.

MIND If you are conscious, and are able to think, feel, have experiences, make decisions, and so on, then you have a mind (though not everything with a mind needs to have *all* these different properties: minds can be unconscious, for example).

MOLECULE A tiny particle made up of atoms.

MORALITY Morality is concerned with right and wrong—with what we should and should not do. For example, most of us believe that repaying one's debts is right and stealing is wrong.

NATURAL SELECTION The process by which evolution occurs. Natural selection is explained in chapter eight.

NEURON A neuron is a type of cell. It looks like this.

Neurons are what our brains are made out of. Each human brain is made up of millions and millions of neurons woven together to form a complex network.

OBSERVATION One observes by means of one's five senses: sight, hearing, touch, taste, and smell.

OCKHAM'S RAZOR The philosophical principle that says that when one is faced with two theories, each of which is otherwise equally well supported by the evidence, one should always choose the *simpler* theory.

PERSONAL IDENTITY The philosophical problem of personal identity is the problem of explaining what makes, say, a certain baby one and the same person as a certain old lady.

PHILOSOPHY The question "What is philosophy?" is itself a philosophical question. Philosophers disagree about what philosophy is. In this book I have tried to give you a feel for what philosophy is by giving you examples of the kind of questions philosophers struggle with.

PHYSICAL MATTER Physical matter is made up of atoms and molecules. Physical matter is what physical objects such as a peanut, a chair, this piece of paper, your body, or a galaxy are made out of.

PHYSICAL OBJECT An object made out of physical matter, such as a peanut, a chair, this piece of paper, your body, or a galaxy.

PHYSICAL UNIVERSE The universe that we observe around us and that science focuses on. The only matter in the physical universe is physical matter.

PHYSICAL WORLD See PHYSICAL UNIVERSE.

PLANET A planet is a large object circling a star. Unlike stars, planets don't give out any light of their own. Earth is a planet.

PROPERTY Objects have properties. For example, my desk is an object that has the following properties: it is made of wood, it is brown, and it weighs ten pounds.

QUALITY See PROPERTY.

REASON You and I can both *reason*: we can think and work things out. We also talk about having a *reason to believe* something. A reason to believe is something that *supports* that belief, makes the belief more likely to be true.

REINCARNATION If you believe in reincarnation, you believe that after a person dies they can be reborn with a new body, perhaps even the body of a different sort of animal.

SAMENESS—QUALITATIVE AND NUMERICAL In the chapter Can I Jump In the Same River Twice? I distinguish two sorts of sameness: numerical and qualitative. Two objects are qualitatively the same if they share all *the same qualities*. Objects are numerically the same if they are *one and the same object*.

SCIENCE System of knowledge arrived at by means of observation and experiment.

SKEPTICISM Skeptics claim that we don't know what we might think we know. For example, skeptics about the external world say that you have no knowledge of the world around you.

SOUL By a soul I mean a supernatural object made out of non-physical matter: "soul stuff." A soul is capable of existing on its own quite independently of anything in the physical universe. According to those who believe in the existence of souls, it is your soul that thinks, feels, is conscious, has experiences, makes decisions, and so on.

STAR Large shining heavenly object. The nearest star to us is the sun. Stars are clustered together to form galaxies.

SUPERNATURAL Not part of the natural, physical universe.

UNIVERSE See PHYSICAL UNIVERSE.

VEGETARIAN Someone who doesn't eat meat.

VEGAN Someone who doesn't eat any animal products.

VIRTUAL ENVIRONMENT The environment to be found within a virtual reality.

VIRTUAL OBJECT An object found within a virtual environment.

VIRTUAL REALITY A computer-generated reality, such as the kind of reality one finds in many computer games.